MY FIRST 100 YEARS!

A Look Back from the Finish Line

By
R. WALDO McBURNEY

Fifth printing November 2005
Fourth printing May 2005
Third printing January 2005
Second printing October 2004.

ISBN: 1-58597-269-X

Library of Congress Control Number: 2004094032

LEATHERS
PUBLISHING
4500 College Blvd.
Overland Park, KS 66211
1/888/888/7696
www.leatherspublishing.com

ACKNOWLEDGMENTS

My daughter, Ruth Mann, has done the typing and first time editing of my manuscript. It meant reading my poor penmanship and copying several times after editing.

Others who have helped in various ways are Kenneth McBurney, Virginia McBurney, Wendell McBurney and Lorraine Forman. My wife Vernice has been my faithful and patient encourager through the years I have been working on this book. Many others have kept reminding and urging me to hurry up with the book.

My wish is that readers will be encouraged by my story, which most likely will be my last one.

SOME FAVORITE BITS OF WISDOM

- *"Use it or lose it."*

- *"Motion is the best joint lotion."*

- *"Run for your life."*

- *"You are what you eat."*

- *"My food is my medicine and my medicine is my food."*

Question: *When are you going to retire?"*
Answer: *"When I go out there."*
          (pointing toward cemetery)

"You seem always the same age, never growing older."
                        — daughter Ruth Mann

"The Lord is my Shepherd."
                                        — Psalm 23:1

"The Lord is my Strength."
                                        — Exodus 15:2

"You are not your own; you are bought with a price."
                                        — I Corinthians 6:20

CONTENTS

INTRODUCTION

"Are you still running?" This is a question I am asked repeatedly — even by people from far and near that I can't name. My answer varies. It has been simply, "Yes," or "Not since this morning," or "Yes, but in my old age I'm walking instead of running."

Some ask to what I attribute my length of life. Most people assume it is because I have continued to run. Some would suggest that it is because I eat honey, or I eat right. Others say it is a gift of God. As I look for my own answer, I think of things that may have contributed to quality and length of life. To start right, "I must have picked my parents with great care." But, of course, I didn't pick my parents or choose the genes I wanted — God did this. So my list of answers is long.

Why I have been able to run and produce thousands of pounds of honey is a question people tend to answer in their own way. The answer, I think, is too simplified, like, I can still run because I eat honey, or I can run because I keep on running. One fact I am fairly sure about is that if I hadn't been a distance runner since 65 years of age, I wouldn't be keeping 100 colonies of bees and processing the honey, past 100 years of age. Likewise, I wouldn't have been able to operate a seed cleaning service to age 91 without continued running. Another man who operated a cleaner, but sold it, said, "It takes the stamina of a young man to run a seed cleaner."

Gold medals in ten track and field events in national and world competitions until I was past 100 are evidence of special training in other basics besides exercise.

My neighbor, Bob Severance, of Beloit, Kansas, who produced and sold unpasteurized milk, had a son, Wilford, who proved to be very healthy in a school physical examination. On being asked why he was so healthy, he replied, "Because I don't eat spinach, and I don't drink pasteurized milk!"

I can make some definite statements that I believe have been contributing factors in my continued strength. I name just a few here.

The true answer to continued strength is many-fold. It includes not only exercise and nutrition, but psychological attitudes, spiritual faith, rest, inherited genes, care of physical and mental stresses, and abstinence from harmful substances, and other influences.

There are plenty of books on running as the answer to long life, and others on nutrition. Many nutritionists recognize exercise as necessary for good health. But few recognize the other aspects mentioned above as having any relevance in the stressful lives we all experience. It is my purpose in this writing to expose the importance of some neglected areas of attaining quality and length of life.

There are over 20 items that may have contributed to my longevity. I'll rule out some of them. "A chain is as strong as its weakest link." Another saying is, "You can't find it all in one horse." Our bodies are made up of many parts; and like a chain, the weak or neglected or abused parts may be our downfall.

Medical doctors saved my life when I had appendicitis at age 58. Fifty years earlier, appendicitis was very often fatal. Again at 87, when I was diagnosed with colon cancer, medical doctors saved my life. My grandmother died in the 1920s with an undiagnosed intestinal problem. My cousin, Dr. F.W. Huston, a medical doctor, said it was colon cancer. Without modern technology, colon cancer might have been my terminal illness.

Good nutrition is no doubt a very significant factor

in my good health. Gardening was always part of our family farm in my childhood, and I continued to have a garden all my life. Besides being wholesome exercise, it provides a variety of nutritious produce. Also, we include whole grains, beans, low-fat meat, dairy products, and fresh, canned, frozen and dried fruits and vegetables.

It takes a combination of a lot of good characteristics to make a good teacher, doctor, banker or almost any other occupation. As you read my life's story, you may make up your mind as to some of the important things that have contributed to my athletic and occupational strengths which my friends describe as "phenomenal," "great," "incredible," etc. But these achievements are not the greatest thing in life. The following quote helps my humility and discourages my pride:

"In strength of horse or speed of man
The Lord takes no delight;
But those that fear and trust His love
Are pleasing in His sight."

— Psalm 147:10,11
The Book of Psalms for Singing,
Crown & Covenant Publishing, 1973.

Chapter 1

MOVING FROM THE SODDY

WHEN I FIRST started kicking, I lived in a "soddy" —
a sod house. I have the picture of my mother there, and
I was with her, but they didn't know at that time whether
I was a boy or a girl. Then our new frame house was
finished, and we moved into it. A few weeks after the
move, I was born on October 3, 1902, joining two older
brothers. Two more boys and a sister were added later
to the family. Our home was on a farm three miles south-
east of Quinter, in the high plains of western Kansas,
once referred to as the "Great American Desert."

Tired of dishwashing, the five McBurney brothers
hoped for a baby sister ("dish washer!"). On April 28,
1912, we stopped at the mail box on our way home from
school and read the outgoing mail, which was a post-
card. It announced that our new baby was the longed-
for girl. My father called his cousin, Mae Graham (Mrs.
Elmer), to announce the new arrival. She was anxious
to learn the gender, and my father delayed that information to tantalize her. In desperation, she asked for
the name. The answer was "Sarah John." Finally my father gave the name as Martha Elizabeth, after her two
grandmothers. You can't fully appreciate this episode
without knowing cousin Mae.

In those days a doctor was not always available to
deliver babies. I think my older brothers came with a

doctor's assistance. Mrs. Bowman, a neighbor a mile away, was the mid-wife at the birth of Beth, the youngest in our family. I have no idea whether or not I had a doctor at my birth. They issued no birth certificates in those days in Gove County, Kansas. I finally succeeded in getting one when I was 96 years old.

. It was dresses for boys until about three years old when I was a child. I don't remember that part of my life, but it's true. Then we wore knickerbockers — pants that came just below the knee — and they were a pain that I remember. They are on my *avoid* list.

Before modern refrigeration methods, people preserved food in ice boxes if they had an ice house (a dugout with a roof) or access to an ice plant. When kitchen water buckets froze over, it was time for the ice harvest. The ice saw, ice tongs and neighbors were gathered, and a trip was made to ponds along the Saline River or Big Creek, or man-made dams. Ice was cut with a saw similar to the cross- cut saw used to cut firewood. When the ice house was filled, the ice was covered with straw for insulation. As needed, ice was put in the icebox in the house for refrigeration.

Some people didn't have this supply of ice. Larger towns often had ice plants that produced ice for sale, and some stores sold ice. People who had no ice house usually could have ice cream only when they got up enough nerve to "borrow" ice from a neighbor with an ice house. Common methods of preserving foods were canning, drying, curing, pickling and storing in caves or pits.

The McBurney farm in Pennsylvania, where my father grew up, had a spring that fed a tank in a small building they called a spring house. This water was the household refrigerator to keep milk, butter, cream, etc., cool. My father made the same arrangement on our Kansas farm, except the water came from the windmill which pumped water from 105 feet underground. He called it a well house. This arrangement, along with the cave, kept things cool in summer and from freezing in winter, except in extreme weather. The cave was a great place to store canned goods and fresh fruits and vegetables. When needed, it served as a tornado cellar. We also rode down the top of it with our sleds and wagons.

Cream and eggs were a common source of income in early days. Small towns often had more than one cream station, where cream, butter, poultry, eggs and hides were marketed. Due to poor refrigeration, much of this produce was of low quality by the time it reached the consumer. Some produce was shipped direct by rail to big produce houses in larger cities.

We five boys all slept in an unfinished upstairs room. Snow and dust sometimes sifted through cracks onto our beds when we had a dust storm, since the roof was not solid sheeted. The dust made its way into our house and covered everything. We didn't bother to light the kerosene lamps when we went to bed. At one time there was a large sack of unshelled peanuts at the head of the stairs, and I often ate peanuts on my way to bed. My taste buds developed until I could tell a wormy peanut in the dark. In later years, I detected the same distinctive flavor in some brands of peanut butter, before Pure Food and Drug interfered. And I still like peanuts!

In real cold weather the heater in the living room was banked to hold the fire overnight. In the morning the flues were opened and the fire took off. The kitchen range didn't hold fire overnight, so it had to be started with kindling. On rare occasions ice formed on the pail that held the drinking water.

My generation lived through measles, whooping cough, mumps, smallpox and chicken pox, since we didn't have all those vaccinations presently "enjoyed" by children. But, of course, some children of that time did *not* survive such diseases. My oldest brother, Wendell, died in 1915 of pneumonia at the age of 17. This was before penicillin and sulfa drugs were available.

We all took baths every Saturday night, whether we needed it or not. Baths were taken in a big round tub — the same "warsh" tub used on Mondays for washing clothes. (We didn't pronounce "wash" properly, as our Pennsylvania cousins did.) The tub was filled with hot water from the reservoir in the back of the kitchen range and an oblong boiler on top of the stove. Previous to 1917, the kitchen was the room in which we washed our hands, fed our faces and bathed. We didn't change the water for each participant. The bathing was done beside the kitchen stove. One time my older brother, Edwin, got too close to the stove and got a burn that left a permanent scar on his tummy. In the summer, a swim in the stock water tank was sometimes a substitute.

Since there was no sink or drain in the house, all our water had to be carried into and out of the house. We drank from a pitcher hanging near a bucket of water. When the water pail became empty, it meant a trip to the well outside. If the wind wasn't blowing, the well had to be pumped by hand.

When we moved to Sterling, Kansas, in 1917, our home there had a regular bathroom and bathtub. We pumped water with a pitcher pump in the kitchen and carried it to the bathtub, along with stove-heated water.

Other conveniences that are included in our present-day bathrooms were out behind the house (in Quinter) in a small building. A pit was under the seat, which had two or three holes in it.

I have no memory of toothbrushes in those days, and I don't remember any bedtime orders to brush our teeth. In spite of this "neglect," I have all but my wisdom teeth today. I have come to believe that brushing is not the main secret in having good teeth. Perhaps fluoride in the drinking water is a stronger factor.

On Sunday, we were always in church. That morning, there was more than the usual urgency about getting the "cow-milkers" out of bed, the horses, cows and chickens fed, the cows milked, cream separated, and the separator washed. Then came breakfast and family worship.

Next, the horses had to be harnessed and hitched to the spring wagon. It had no side curtains or lights. We had heavy lap robes and sometimes hot bricks to keep our feet warm. Some neighbors had surreys with side curtains.

We counted on a half-hour to get to church in Quinter, three miles from our farm. Sometimes the horses were covered with blankets, as they were tied to hitching posts while still hitched to the vehicles. In cold weather the horses were cooled off after standing for two hours, and they took off at a brisk pace to warm up as they headed for home. The moon usually shines brightly in western Kansas, but one night we couldn't see. My father let the team of horses find the way home. They stopped one time, supposedly to get their bearings, then took us on home safely.

In later years, as automobiles came without self-starters, it was the man who pulled the crank in front of the car who got warmed up! The radiator was sometimes drained, or blanketed, to prevent freezing. Who wants the "good old days"?

Monday was always wash day. It was only that one day a week, not just whenever you needed clean clothes, as it often is now. Just as on Saturday bath night, the wash water had to be carried into the house, heated on the stove, then carried back outdoors when the washing was finished. The bath tub became the wash tub. White clothes were often boiled clean. Other clothes were cleaned over the wash board, which was a job for an adult. The clean clothes were put through a wringer, temporarily attached to the side of the wash tub. This wringer is a hand-cranked machine with two rubber rollers. Drying was finished on outdoor clotheslines exposed to the Kansas wind and sun. In freezing weather, they were hung on temporary lines in the house.

If it was raining in western Kansas, the damp clothes could wait — "the sun will be out in ten minutes" — as some old-timers would say.

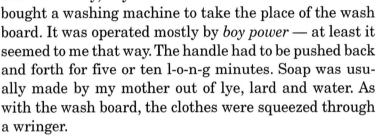

In the early days of the 20th century, my folks bought a washing machine to take the place of the wash board. It was operated mostly by *boy power* — at least it seemed to me that way. The handle had to be pushed back and forth for five or ten l-o-n-g minutes. Soap was usually made by my mother out of lye, lard and water. As with the wash board, the clothes were squeezed through a wringer.

When our socks got holes in them, we didn't throw them in a trash bag. They were darned and kept in use. Floyd Crist, in his booklet, *Farm Machinery*, tells about Horace Putoff, a single farmer, who said that he darned his socks repeatedly until they were all darn from top to toe.

Flour and sugar were often sold in 50-pound sacks made of cloth. When empty, the sacks were sometimes made into underwear. A little later, feed came in colored print sacks, which were commonly sewn into dresses or play clothes.

Tuesday was ironing day. Clothes in those days had to be ironed to look right — no "permapress" fabrics then. Corn starch was often used to add stiffness to dress clothes. One type of iron had a non-removable handle. If the family budget could handle it, we could have a removable handle and two irons. One iron would be heating on the kitchen range while the hot one was being used. The heat in the stove made it a good time for baking on Tuesday, also.

The rest of the week was free for other activities, which were numerous in homes where most of the family food supply was produced and processed. Daily chores on the farm, such as driving cows in from the pasture, milking cows, separating milk, washing the separator, feeding calves, gathering eggs, feeding chickens, filling lamps with kerosene, cleaning lamp chimneys, and carrying in water from the windmill, were done by the whole family. If we wanted fried chicken, we caught the chicken, killed, scalded, plucked the feathers, dressed, and then cooked it like we do today. Everyone had other jobs to do also, which were done without being asked, begged, threatened or argued, without excuses, allowances or minimum wages. (Washing dishes might possibly be an exception to the above performance standard.)

Ten hours was a work day, and six days was a work week in the early 20th century. Most people were farmers and set their own time of work. Hard work hadn't been replaced by labor-saving equipment. When Saturday came, they were ready for the day of rest.

When I went to town, I was bored if I had to wait too long to return home. It was more exciting on the farm, where we hunted rabbits and rattlesnakes, trapped skunks, and played with wagons and sleds which my father made for us. One sled was called a "yankee jumper." What's that? It's a one-runnered sliding machine, made by mounting a milk stool on a barrel stave. It gave quite a thrilling ride, once we mastered it. My father also made a set of harness, starting with the whole cow hide.

When I was a boy, I knew nothing about an allowance. A common way for us to earn money was to trap pocket gophers and skunks. The county paid a five-cent bounty for gopher scalps, which we sent to Gove to collect our bounties. I wonder if the postal people would accept such a shipment now! (I don't remember the cost of postage stamps then, but I do know they were up to 3 cents in the '30s.)

Skunk fur prices ranged from $1.50 to $3.00. The prices depended on whether the furs were broad stripe, narrow stripe or short stripe. The five-cent bounty on gophers sounds small, but some of our church young people paid their way to church camp with that money.

We grew up in a house with an organ, two violins and a guitar. Our father could play all the instruments. He taught " do re mi" to our school and to the church people. What did I play? The harmonica — after I was out of college! It has been a source of pleasure to this day. My brother Wendell sang and chorded for himself on the organ. I had hoped to have as good a voice as his, but it didn't happen. On a July 4th picnic at the Bailey grove, we were rained out. When we retreated to the house, Wendell entertained us by singing and playing. He sang in the high school male quartet, with Floyd Crist, Louis Bowman and Curtis Bowman. (These are the names as I recall, but I couldn't confirm this from the 1915 yearbook.)

Miles on foot were no problem in those days. One day several school-aged boys walked through our farmstead. They had come from Elmer Long's a mile south and were headed for Wolf's a mile north.

Telephones came along in the first decade of the century, but many people didn't have them at first. About six families would be on one line. We could call people on our own line directly, but we had to go through "central" (later called "operator") to be connected with people on other lines. The signals were in long and short rings. For example, our ring might be a long and two shorts, or some other combination.

"Rubbering" on the phone lines was a common habit. You could lift the receiver and hear other people's conversations. It was customary when making a call to lift the receiver and ask, "Is the line busy?" If the line was busy too long, a person with an urgent call would ask for the line. If too many rubberers were on the line, the reception was so poor that the caller would have to ask people to hang up. When it was baby chick season, it was a busy time with baby chick talk. One time a rubberer was heard to say, "Johnny, get off the table!" This was a give-away as to her identity!

Mothers didn't look for a job in town in the horse and buggy days. My mother had six children to look after, and didn't have the labor-saving devices of today. She had fast hands and could get a lot of work done in a day. She made soap, brewed vinegar, canned fruits, vegetables and meat, dried fruits, put up sauerkraut, churned cream into butter, washed, ironed and mended clothes, raised a garden and cooked meals.

Mother was also our barber. One summer day, she placed me on a stool in the shade of the house to cut my hair with hand clippers. She left me for a few minutes to chase a chicken out of the garden. While she was gone I helped her cut my hair. I couldn't understand why she didn't appreciate my help.

For the service of those who didn't have a barber in the family, the town barbers had a long Saturday. The straight-edge razor was the shaving instrument. The shaving mug and soap were round, and a lather was made with a shaving brush. A little piece of salt peter was usually handy to stop any bleeding that came from nicks or scratches. A skillful shaver seldom needed this. A leather strap was hanging nearby to use in keeping the razor in cutting condition. No safety or electric razors were available. I had a straight-edge razor, but I never became skilled in its use before I got a safety razor.

When we were a little picky at the dinner table, my father would say, "Eat what's set before you, asking no questions for conscience sake." I think he took this Bible verse a little out of context, but it saved Mother from taking orders cafe style, and saved food from being dumped in the garbage for the chickens and cats. We didn't waste food. My father often remarked at the dinner table, "Chew your food; your stomach has no teeth." Brother Paul restated it this way, "Chew your food; your stomach ain't got no teeth!"

On April 20, 1910, we planned to celebrate brother Edwin's tenth birthday by ducking (currently called "dunking") him in the stock water tank. He declined and went over the hill to the prairie dog town. He raced back to tell us that he had found a rattlesnake. Forgetting the ducking, we armed ourselves with hoes and went for the big kill. We killed three rattlesnakes and had a happy birthday without a ducking.

One day when our parents were gone, we decided to learn whether or not heat would blow the cork out of an oil can. It did! A spray of oily water blew the cork out and sprayed the mess on the ceiling of our summer kitchen. It dripped down over a basket of clothes. Our parents didn't mention the incident. They probably were glad we didn't blow up the house.

One day Mother got tricky about serving pie. She first served us an extra special big meal, then presented us each with a whole pie! She grinned as we strained to stuff the whole thing down.

My brother Edwin and I devised an experiment to determine if a barrel hoop could be straightened. Edwin stood on one end of the hoop and I on the other. We had it straight for a moment, until he stepped off his end. The springing hoop hit me just above the left eye. I'm thankful that I am not blind in one eye.

In early days, our church encouraged us to sign a pledge to abstain from the use of tobacco and alcoholic beverages. I signed this pledge and have kept it during my entire life. My parents told us that tobacco was bad and that cigarettes were *worse*. A mystery to me is how my parents knew this before 1910, but many people haven't learned it until they approach death at an early age from heart trouble, lung cancer, emphysema or other tobacco-related ailments.

We were blessed with good neighbors, who came to our aid in many ways. One time when my father was away from home, we had trouble with our well. In order to pull the pipes, we needed to know how to make the hitch with rope that secured the pipe. We asked Henry Wolf for help. He walked a mile to show us how to tie it. I have since known that knot as the clove hitch.

Help often came without the aid of telephones. When my brother Wendell died in 1915, Henry Wolf came and asked what he could do for us. My father told him we needed a load of straw for bedding. With the assistance of myself and a brother or two, we hitched up the horses, went to the straw stack and got the straw. That was a very practical way to help our family.

In 1910 when Henry Wolf was building his house, he also built a little out-house for the convenience of the carpenters. After building it, he hoed the weeds around it. When asked if he expected the building to grow, he replied, "Yes, it will be growing stronger!"

After we bought our first family car in 1917, we took a long trip to Blanchard, Iowa, a distance of about 425 miles from Quinter. We pitched our tent for overnight stops along the way. It took five days to get there, at our speed limit of an unbelievable 20 mph, and we slowed down for the corners. (Corners were corners in those days, not curves.)

My father had a stroke in 1914, and a more serious stroke in 1916, while at a family reunion in Estes Park, Colorado. The loss of my father's health and the death of brother Wendell led to the sale of the Quinter farm. It was sold in 1917 to Elder D.A. Crist, and has since been occupied by his children and grandchildren, to the fourth generation.

My parents then purchased a 15-acre tract near Sterling, Kansas. The change was a shock to me. Since I was known in boyhood as a gardener, my mother comforted me by telling me that we could grow almost anything at Sterling. There, we had irrigation for truck gardening and fruit-growing. Alfalfa supported a team of horses and a cow or two. My father's recovery from the stroke was good. He didn't recover his full previous capacity, but for many years he could look after the horses, cows, chickens, garden and orchard.

By the end of the 20th century, vast changes had been made in rural communities. Big machinery and larger farms had made life different. It was a rare farm on which chickens and pigs were raised, and cows were milked. Large specialized farms had taken over these projects with modern methods. Everybody had become dependent on electricity and modern equipment. If terrorists were to blow up power plants, it would cause chaos.

With modern equipment, stockmen can feed 100 cattle in less time than it would take to milk one cow, separate the milk and wash the cream separator. So they buy dairy products at the grocery store. Many farm wives work at jobs in town and buy their groceries, instead of selling cream and eggs. I was slow in adjusting to this change, since farmers are "supposed" to produce their own food. Gardening became a lost art in many homes, as fresh produce is available year-round in grocery stores.

Chapter 2

RUNNING TO SCHOOL

IT ISN'T THE reading, writing and arithmetic my teachers taught that I remember, but the extras they were not paid to do. Their giving of self scored with me.

Our country school sometimes had students in all eight grades. The teacher was not only an instructor, but a janitor, heating engineer, water carrier, recreation director, coach, disciplinarian and nurse. They did all of this for $20 to $30 a month!

Joe Bowman and Blanche Woodward were my early teachers. Cecil Calvert taught when grown boys still went to school. He was equal to the occasion and handled all eight grades with military precision. I well remember the day in the fall of 1911, after the national election, when he came to school saying, "Hurrah for Woodrow Wilson!" Partly due to that, I have always remembered that President Wilson took office in 1912.

Sam Long supplied drawing paper we could use when we had finished our lessons. This I enjoyed. He invited us to his home one night so his wife could teach us some new songs. Pauline Green, who later married Walter Maxwell, came from a musical family. She taught us songs that few kids had the opportunity to learn.

When Sam Ebbert taught, we were introduced to basketball. Our basketball court had a buffalo grass floor and the advantages of outdoor air. We played the

Fairview school west of Quinter, but I don't remember who won. Other games that we enjoyed were baseball, "Pump, Pump, Pull Away" and "Fox and Goose" when the ground was snow-covered. I appreciated Sam's good coaching, but I was displeased that he had us eat our lunches in our seats inside instead of outside on the south side of the building as we formerly had done. This was an infringement on personal liberty, in my seventh grade mind.

Drinking water came from a hand pump outside the school house. We had a three-gallon pail beside the door and a long-handled dipper, from which everyone drank. The time finally came when Elizabeth Wooster, state superintendent of public instruction, insisted on individual drinking cups. I don't recall having a towel or wash basin.

Literary society meetings were common in the early days of the 20th century, which met in country school houses. Ciphering and spelling matches, as well as songs, readings, debates and dialogues, were the entertainment. At one meeting of a literary society, a man presented a subject he wished to hear debated: "Resolved, that a long rat with a short tail can get through a hole quicker than a short rat with a long tail." One time our teacher, Cecil Calvert, was ciphering with his former teacher. The problem was in multiplication in which one could either multiply by .25 or divide by 4 to get the answer. Cecil got the answer without copying on the blackboard, then gazed at his opponent, and finally wrote it down and read it just ahead of her. He announced that she had taught him this short cut (dividing by 4 instead of multiplying by .25).

We McBurneys walked one and a half miles to school. The Wolfs, Lahmans, Knauses and some others were over two miles from school. Some rode or drove horses to school. Sometimes we worked our trap lines on the way to school, which wasn't good if we caught a skunk!

No one came to our country school with skunk odors we couldn't tolerate. When I was in high school, we had a serious incident. One Monday morning, a strong skunk odor permeated the school building. Classes were dismissed for the day. The superintendent thought there must have been a break-in. The state inspector happened to arrive that day, to add to the embarrassment!

I got the rest of the story several years later from a girl who had dated one of the culprits. According to his account to her, two boys entered the unlocked building while the school board was meeting. They lifted the grate of a heat duct and dropped in the musk sack of a skunk. The school board was meeting on the same floor. Unsuspecting, the superintendent asked one of the two boys to act as a detective to find out who was guilty. The other boy was president of the "HiY." How could two highly respected boys do such a thing? This happened in Sterling High School.

Different ages of students sometimes brought some problems. My younger brother Paul was throwing a croquet ball and catching it. Another boy, seven years older, attempted to catch it, and the ball hit Paul and broke his tooth. On another occasion, the older boy was taking advantage of Paul, I thought, so I whacked him on the bottom and broke my stick. He took after me and chased me into the school house. The teacher told us to sit down, and we obeyed and cooled off.

One day, I was standing alone when a big boy came along and knocked my feet out from under me. I fell flat and had a headache the rest of the day. I didn't tell the teacher. That event gave me a bad feeling toward bullies. The problem with bullies didn't end with the country school.

Chapter 3

COMING TO MATURITY

AFTER HIGH SCHOOL in Sterling, Kansas, I attended Sterling College for two years, then transferred to Kansas State Agricultural College, now called Kansas State University, in Manhattan, Kansas. It had 4,000 students at that time, which included about 3,000 men and 1,000 women.

Odds were against me in locating a future wife. Would you like to know how I met her? The day before enrollment, I was at a church in Eskridge. A woman there told me about her nephew, Norman Spear, who was attending K-State. Then she sort of incidentally said that his sister was also going to K-State. Immediately I was more interested in the niece than the nephew!

On registration day, I was strolling on the campus with hundreds of others, when a man called to me, and then apologized, saying he was looking for Norman Spear. I told him that I, too, was looking for Norman Spear. The man was Wallace Benson, who later became my roommate, and a generation later his son became my son's roommate. He told me to go to the United Presbyterian church Friday night and I would meet Norman Spear. I went, and met not only Norman, but his sister, Irene, who became my wife four years later.

Can you believe this story — with 3,000 men on campus and meeting someone who was looking for the same man I was looking for? How do you account for such an odd event? (Hint!) I know my parents were praying for me, for they always did.

My college roommate, Albert Haltom, encouraged me to go out for cross-country. Later in my college life I encouraged my roommate, Wallace Benson, to go out for cross-country. Verle Oline was my other roommate. They all had a good influence on me. I needed their input to help me grow up right. All of us later married and had families. Today I am the only one living out of the four couples. I am in contact with children of two of these roommates.

I ran to and from classes when I was in college in Sterling and Manhattan. I practiced some with the cross-country team at K-State with no intentions of making the team. I did it because I enjoyed running. It was a privilege to be acquainted with the members of the cross country team. This team all came in abreast ahead of the other teams in one race. Those team members were Paul Axtell, Leslie Moody, Ralph Kimport, Myron Sallee and Temple Winburn. I was not in the class with those elite runners.

I graduated from Kansas State in 1927, with horticulture as my major, and was qualified to teach vocational agriculture. I married my college sweetheart, Irene Spear, in 1929. Over the next 11 years , we had three children — Kenneth, Ruth and Mary Jane.

My first three years out of college were spent as a vocational agriculture teacher in Beloit, Kansas, and the next 17 years as County Agricultural Agent in Beloit and Hill City, Kansas. During those years, vitamins were being discovered, and my work kept me in contact with discoveries through specialists in livestock and human nutrition.

At the 4-H Roundup in Manhattan, the dairy specialist tried to get me to drink a glass of milk at all three meals. I got the breakfast glass down, then balked on the other two glasses. I told the specialist that if cows could get calcium out of grass, so could I. He said, "Well, you could if you had four stomachs!" I have not been much of a milk consumer since age five. I used my sound teeth as evidence to support my anti-milk practice. My teeth have been small, and if I were a sheep I would classify as a "short mouth." Actually, though I'm a little hard on milk, because of my personal taste, I recognize it as a very good and essential food, especially for children.

I had three years of work with the Midwest Cooperative in Quinter, Kansas. After this, I went to self-employment. My work involved more physical labor than the previous 24 years since college graduation. It included several seasonal projects. Seed processing on the farm was the main one, along with increased beekeeping as a part-time enterprise, and sharpening disks. The last one I took on was income tax preparation, which occupied my winters. Income tax was the first enterprise that I dropped. That was followed by disk sharpening. I cleaned seed for 41 years, until I was 91. I still keep bees, even though honey seems to get "heavier" year by year as old age and weakness gradually take their toll.

After thirty good years of marriage, my wife Irene died of leukemia in 1960. I got married two years later, to Vernice Chestnut Forman, who has been my wonderful companion and co-worker. We celebrated our 40th anniversary in 2002.

Vernice's three sons — Rhea, John and Tom Forman — were added to my three children to make up our combined family. All six children are married, and have given us 18 grandchildren and 25 great-grandchildren.

Sometimes people ask me what I consider to be the best age of my life. I have replied, "Whatever age I am is the best age!" When I got my first gray hairs, I maintained that "gray hair is a sign of distinction." When I turned forty, I quoted the saying, "Life begins at forty." Each age has its pleasures, along with problems and challenges. I thank God for each day and year.

Chapter 4

STARVING AMERICA

MY FATHER HAD a stroke in 1914 and another one in 1916. He was treated for several months by his brother, Dr M.R. McBurney, in California, who was a medical doctor and a chiropractor. When my father came home, he didn't come with pills and prescriptions.

He came teaching us that we should eat lots of fruits, vegetables, whole grain cereals and beans. He lived over 30 years after his stroke, to age 88. This gave me a high respect for good nutrition. He came home with a book, *Starving America,* written by Alfred W. McCann, published in 1912. Mother read much of this book to the family. I don't know what happened to this book, but our local library recently got a copy for me from a California university library.

This book emphasizes the harm done by removing most of the minerals from wheat and feeding that part of the kernel to livestock. He wrote that 75 percent of the minerals in vegetables are lost when cooked and the water poured down the drain. McCann claimed that processing of grains such as polishing, pearling and bolting, takes away 75 percent of the minerals. McCann said that many people believe that meat is a complete food. It is not, he wrote, unless you eat the blood and bones. He suggested that grocery stores should sell cornmeal containing all the corn, including the part usually fed to hogs. Another quote: "GOD put 12 vitalizing mineral salts into the wheat. MAN takes eight of them out in order to make flour white and then wonders why there are so many false teeth."

When I was in college and doing some cooking, I remembered what I had learned from *Starving America*. Three of us — Albert Haltom, Verle Oline and I — took weekly turns at cooking. Using the principle that many of the minerals in vegetables come out in the boiling water, I used the potato water in making gravy. Then I also used the turnip water for the oatmeal. That didn't meet approval! That was my prize bonehead.

McCann saw America starving before 1912. What would he see today? He would see that one of four children is overweight and one of three adults is overweight. He would see families growing up without a garden and not getting enough fruits and vegetables, even though they are available at the grocery store and they are financially able to buy them. He would see students riding to school when they don't get their exercise from sports or physical education class. He would see this even in my small town where we don't have the danger of kidnappers. He would see pop and candy machines in the school buildings. It would "blow his mind" to see the things that some people carry home from the grocery store. He wouldn't be surprised that they are overweight and having heart by-passes, strokes and cancer.

McCann's book was written before there was knowledge of vitamins. It is amazing to note how nearly all of his recommendations fit into the present-day dietary recommendations to avoid heart trouble, strokes, cancer, diabetes, arthritis and obesity. Some of his statements would not be proved by later research. Today, I think he would put more emphasis on fats, and he would know about the value of vitamins.

My father's experience has led me to a life-long interest in nutrition. I have read everything that came in sight on the subject. I have had great trouble sorting out the true from the false. My study in livestock feeding at Kansas State University gave me some basic information, much of which applies to human nutrition. Through my years in Agricultural Extension work and my association with foods, poultry and livestock specialists, I was able to keep up with many scientific discoveries.

It is encouraging to see a decrease in heart trouble and strokes recently because many people are following better life styles. Only 8% of our population has taken up consistent exercise programs. We are not about to reach 120 years of age, which some claim is a possibility. Not many, including me, are willing to pay the price. I tend to do what I have to do to keep in relatively good shape, but no more!

Some people seem indifferent toward learning what it takes to maintain good health, or they are not willing to do what is necessary. Most of us tend to wait until we have health problems or serious illness, and then expect our doctors to cure us, without taking responsibility for preventive practices. A better way is to follow a preventive lifestyle and avoid bad habits. The best way to lower our health costs is prevention.

Chapter 5

RUNNING FOR LIFE

WHEN DID I start running? When my son Kenneth overheard me telling someone that I started running at age 65, he objected, "Oh, you never stopped running!" He was right, because I have always enjoyed walking and running. But it was also true that I revived distance running at 65.

Henry "Hank" Iba, long-time, highly successful basketball coach at Oklahoma A&M (now Oklahoma State University), noted the apparent increase in knee problems in basketball players, and attributed the problems to lack of exercise. He said, "Today's boy will not walk a quarter mile a day; your boy won't, and my boy won't."

Why have I had no knee problems, except from jumping off and on a 15-inch-high platform in my honey processing room? This hasn't interfered with my athletic activities. From Coach Iba's opinion, I must have had something in my background or active life that gave me a solid make-up.

You should recognize my lack of athletic ability and reputation when I tell you I wasn't good enough to make my high school football team that lost a game 105 to 0! But I have always been physically active, starting with doing my share of chores on the farm in my early years. My youth was filled with heavy physical activities, such as shocking wheat bundles and pitching wheat on thresh-ing and harvest crews. At a weight of 92 pounds at age of 16, I had my first harvest job of shocking wheat for a neighbor, William Hutcheson, in Sterling, Kansas. A middle-aged man started with me. We two were supposed to keep up with the binder. He got sick after the first day and I went ahead alone. By the time the binder had done enough to start shocking in the next field, I was through with the first field and was ready to start the second one. I kept up with the binder, which was all that is expected of anyone, so I got a man's wages, which was 45 cents an hour. I worked only 9 hours a day, for $4. A day's work in 1918 was 10 hours, and a week was 60 hours.

My acquaintance with drudgery, endurance and hard work may be the background resulting in my underpin-ning to serve me well as I went into my late 90s. (Under-pinning is a term used in referring to a horse's legs.)

I walked a mile and a half to school — no rides. That was after milking two or three cows and helping to feed them when I got big enough. On one occasion I was on a Boy Scout hike of about 12 miles round-trip. This was done with 20 paces running and 20 paces walking. In the upper grades and high school at Sterling, we walked and ran to school, usually with our neighbors, the Hutchesons — Wilma, Winnifred and Tom. We ran faster if we got a late start.

A new day came when I read a review of Dr. Kenneth Cooper's book, *Aerobics*, which was printed in the *Read-ers' Digest* in 1968. I was 65 years old at the time. Before that time, I would sneak in a short dash after dark, when nobody was looking. I later purchased Dr. Cooper's book, which not only started me jogging, but influenced nu-merous people in many parts of the world to start run-ning. (Faster than a nine-minute mile is considered "run-ning," and slower is called "jogging.")

The every-day runs brought many and varied experiences. My first running was on the high school track, which was dirt with occasional Mexican sandburs. Perhaps we took to it because it was behind the school buildings, out of view of the general public. The reason for this choice might have been to avoid being seen by people who would fear that some of us old men would fall over dead of a heart attack for doing such vigorous exercise! Several other men were jogging at this time, including Glen Fruth, Charles Archer, Marvin Unruh and Robert Bugbee.

No women were in this group of pioneer joggers. In later years it was learned that fast walking had as much health benefits as jogging, with less impact on joints. With that encouragement, women took up walking. They have been more faithful in exercising than men, it seems to me.

When I started jogging more than one or two miles, and others dropped out, I took to the country roads, where I went 1.5 to 4.5 miles on my workouts. My diary notes remind me of some of the experiences and conditions. These include "head pain next morning," "pain in calf," "cramps after cooling," "legs sluggish," "ankle pain," "buttocks sag"and "still stiff." Pain in the quadriceps led me to jogging backward as a cure, during part of my workout. This gave relief after a few weeks. Weather conditions also got into the diary notes, such as "sprinkling," "snowing," "raining," "slushy," "wet" and "mud."

I was cautioned by friends and warned about the dangers of dying of a heart attack if I ran at my age. The directions included getting a doctor's approval before starting. I didn't. I was told not to run in freezing weather or I'd freeze my lungs. I knew better, before I was told that, because I had run in near-zero weather. After a two-mile jog on February 2, 1978, the temperature was recorded at 10 below zero. (That was before I was old enough to know better.) Anyway, my lungs didn't freeze, as one health professional warned might happen.

The odd fact is that I got no encouragement whatever for running, from any person in the health profession. In the years since, heart patients are instructed to exercise rather than being assigned to the rocking chair. It has been years since I have seen the ad for a home escalator saying, "Save Your Heart!" It was over 29 years later, at age 94, that I had a heart attack, and it was of mild severity, leaving no permanent damage.

At the time when jogging became the "in thing," it suited me fine. I was sitting at my desk doing income tax work in winter months. When spring came and there were bees to feed, seed to clean and disks to sharpen, I was too soft for physical work. I needed winter exercise to be in shape for heavy work. Jogging solved the problem.

I had the idea that when the season came for work that involved physical exercise, that jogging was not important. I finally realized that that kind of work didn't take the place of strenuous exercise for physical fitness. It helps, but it's not adequate. I did discover, though, that I didn't lose much fitness during seed processing season, as that involved more physical exertion.

The aerobics book made the claim that people of any age could work up to running distances. Dr. Cooper's later books have classified running after age 60 as not recommended. Walking has become recognized as a very desirable exercise. Following directions for beginning runners, I would stop for a walk break when I couldn't talk freely. There was a time that I wondered why I ever started running. Some stop running when that feeling hits. I was thrilled when I could run a mile without a walk break. I came to the point that I asked myself,"Why do I need a rest break?" From then on, I didn't stop to walk. I ran up to five miles at a time in races. Instructions said you can run one and a half times what you can handle on a regular basis. For example, when you run a mile with no problems, you can handle one and a half miles. I kept increasing miles until I could do five or six miles. Although I could run 10 kilometers (6.2 miles), I never ran over five miles except in races. I found that this rule applies as I increased miles. If I increased weekly miles more than 10 percent, I could tell that I had over-trained.

Running has many beneficial claims. One is that the body's supply of blood and oxygen will be increased. Arteries will increase in width and capacity. The heart doesn't have to pump as fast. The difference between a pulse of 60 per minute and 50 is over 14,000 beats a day. I have the satisfaction of having a slow heart beat because of running. The cardiovascular system of runners provides a good supply of blood to all parts of the body. It gives strength for better survival in emergencies such as heart attacks or surgery.

In increasing running, the energy (sugar called glycogen) stored in muscle cells is increased to last the distance the runner trains to run. This benefit enabled me to set a state record in Kansas for age 80 in the 10-mile run. I reasoned that if I could run two, five or ten miles, I could work all day without the noon meal, without weakening. I proved the truth of this theory by working all day on my feet without food or weakening.

Strenuous exercise such as running tends to relieve stress. I am a morning exerciser, but many runners working under stress run in the evening to relieve stresses of the day. Exercise stimulates the production of cortisone by the body. According to my reading, this is beneficial as a tranquilizer. I believe this statement, partly from an experience while in college at K-State. I had finished gym class, which consisted of running nearly a mile, and I felt exhilarated. Then my mail from home stated that the chicken house at home had burned down. I had conflicting feelings, in spite of the bad news, but I felt good because of the running.

Regular exercise, whether it's running, walking,

swimming, gardening or other activities, has many benefits in addition to the ones I have already enumerated. The list is long — lowers blood pressure and cholesterol, strengthens bones, limits arthritis, reduces fat, can help prevent or delay heart trouble, cancer and diabetes, strengthens muscles and lungs, aids sleep, and more. Experts advise Americans to get at least 30 minutes of moderately intense exercise three to five days a week.

A common saying among runners is "Use it or lose it." George Sheahan, writing about running, advised people to check with their physicians before beginning. "The most dangerous part of all is watching from the stands" (Page 192, Dr. Sheahan, *On Running*).

My stepson, Rhea Forman, Ph.D. in clinical psychology, told me that my occupational activities were unusual, because they required both mental and physical activities. I asked, "What's wrong with that?" He explained that it was good, because "use it or lose it" applies to the mind as well as the body.

I started running at age 65 because I enjoyed running, and for health reasons. I hoped to live a healthy and useful life, and not be slowed down as my father was. My conscious effort in seeking this was through exercise and nutrition. My goal was reached in that I processed seed until I was 91, and continued bee-keeping after 100.

When I was 87, I visited Dr. Cooper in his clinic in Dallas, Texas. I knew his time was precious, but I told the receptionist I would like to meet Dr. Cooper. She told me his office was at the end of the hall, and he would be coming out for lunch soon. My wife Vernice and friends Joe and Edie Copeland waited for him with me. When he appeared, I introduced myself and told him he had started me running 22 years ago, and I didn't know when to quit. He said, "Don't quit!" He asked me how old I was, and I answered, "Eighty-seven." He gave me one of his books, and I told him I already had it. He gave me another book, and I also had it. The third try was one I didn't have. He autographed that book, entitled, *It's Better to Believe.*

I wrote the following poem about running when I was in my 60s:

THE FUN RUNNER
Here's a fellow out for a run.
He takes it easy and it's great fun.
He may go one, three or ten miles -
He'll be back late but all in smiles.

If challenged to a race,
He can set a fast pace.
His moves are gentle, rhythmic and free,
Whether he's 14, 15 or 83.

Chapter 6

REACHING NEW GOALS

AFTER TEN YEARS of distance running strictly for pleasure and health, I decided to go public and enter races. I had never considered myself an athlete, and I hadn't participated much in competitive sports. I ran for fitness and because I enjoyed running. Entering races turned my fitness program into a sport. That gave me an extra incentive to keep up the program, and I needed that when it was easier to lie in bed than to face a cold wind. Racing brought me in contact with other people with the same "odd" ideas about the "good life."

In my first races I was a little nervous before a race. In later races I was not the least bit excited. I learned that the runners ahead of me didn't appear to be going fast, but their pace was too fast for me. In my first few races I was tempted to start too fast. It was better to follow someone who ran my slower speed. I had a feeling that those in charge of some of the races thought someone should keep an eye on me to see that I didn't collapse. I claimed to be like a mule, and wouldn't hurt myself.

Entering public races for the first time was done with fear and trembling. My first race was a one-hour run at Lacrosse, Kansas. As the race was getting ready to start, the race director asked me how long I had lived in Kansas. I replied, "Seventy-three years," and after a slight pause, I added, "and eight months." I think he was asking for my age in a timid way. I ran six miles and 80 yards in the hour. Some of the young race walkers had gone farther than that.

The second race was a quarter-mile at a Hill City Grade School track meet with a class for adults. Three coaches entered the quarter-mile. Halfway through the race, the overweight runner slowed and I passed him. The grandstand responded with cheers. Only one other man ran with me in the half-mile race. He beat me easily.

The third race I entered was a masters' mile at a college indoor track meet of small colleges, at Fort Hays State College, in Hays, Kansas, when I was 75 years old. I wrote a report of this race for our family, and persuaded my wife Vernice to write a report from a spectator's standpoint. She was surprised to see it printed in *Master Pieces,* a publication of the Mid America Running Association, and the Hays Area Road Runners newsletter. Following are the two reports of that event.

❖❖❖

VIEW OF A SPORTS PARTICIPATOR
by Waldo McBurney

Two years ago, I went to a track meet of small colleges in the new coliseum at Hays, ready to suit up for a masters mile run. I knew I would be lapped three times by the young runners, and I would be running three laps after the race was over. That would be too embarrassing, and besides that, the spectators would know the winners and would have no interest in the slowest runner to appear all evening. They would no doubt head for the door rather than wait around for my finish. Under these circumstances I decided to leave my running gear in the car and go to the balcony to enjoy the meet with Vernice, my wife and date. I met the other master milers, all new acquaintances.

This year I decided to swallow my pride and run even at my slow pace. I would ask the others how I could best keep out of their way as they passed me repeatedly. The building atmosphere was dry and warmer than my near-zero practice trails had been through my winter runs. Running was hard, and my mouth got dry. After the others finished, the crowd made so much noise I couldn't hear Fred Irwin, my pace advisor, call out the time. Two younger runners joined me in my second solo lap out of respect, hope, sympathy, support or encouragement. Whatever the motive, I appreciated this fellowship. I wound up the run with a kick, which was accompanied by cheers from all over the place. I didn't know until afterwards, but the spectators had come to their feet. It was as if someone had revealed how to retain the fountain of youth under the generally accepted handicap of old age.

The reaction of the crowd was a surprise to me. I would prefer that this praise would be directed to the One who created us all in such a fearful and wonderful way.

After the run the time was taken up in interviewing by a news reporter, and receiving congratulations from the college track men and the spectators. The ticket-seller girls who couldn't believe that I was one of the runners acted a little sheepish.

About the time we got up the next morning, a Hays paper, to which we do not subscribe, was brought to our door. It had pictures and a story of the meet. The headline was, "Fort Hays Wins Meet; McBurney Wins Crowd." Since then dozens of people in the home town have spoken approvingly. Friends have brought and mailed papers to us so we could share them with other friends and relatives.

I trust that this experience will be instrumental in helping people become aware of the marvelous potential of the human body and help motivate each one to care for it with all diligence and thankfulness.

VIEW OF A SPECTATOR
by Vernice McBurney

We looked forward to a fun evening, and it proved to be just that.

Fred Irwin, a counselor at the Quinter High School with some training in P.E., his wife Suzanne, Deanne, six, and Katie, two, drove us to Hays. We snacked, but Waldo couldn't eat after 4 p.m. until after the run, when we all went out for pizza.

The evening went quickly but, of course, we had our eye on one certain event — the Masters mile. As the four lined up to run, we saw that the one we were most interested in was on the inside lane. The other runners had given him the favorite spot. When the gun went off, our favorite went into what looked like an easy stride and kept that pace. Edie Copeland had joined us, and she kept saying, "It is too hot in here for Waldo to run." He didn't show it, and we didn't know until afterward it had been much harder than outdoor running.

When the announcer announced the names for the master mile and gave Waldo's age, the first cheer went up, and it didn't really subside until the race was over. We heard only one remark. About halfway through the run, a person across the aisle said, "Well, he is still going." On the last lap, you could see the people rising and clapping as he went around until most of the people were on their feet.

We had no idea there would be such a reception. I wish you all could have been there to see and hear the cheers. I, probably more than anyone else, appreciated the response he got, because I knew the diligence and discipline required in his fitness program. I, too, want to give the praise and thanks to God that he has given Waldo the physical ability to glorify Him in his running.

I have since recognized that people respect a distance finisher regardless of age. Late finishers were cheered like the winners, and they are considered winners when they finish the race, having done their best. When I entered a road race with 25, 50 or 300 entrants in my 70's, I didn't expect to come in near the front. Neither did I expect to come in last. The last ones to finish were cheered like the fastest even if they couldn't keep up with an "old" man like me. My objective was always to finish and that was the objective of the others. Some may run to show a pessimistic friend that they can finish. The objective of many runners is to maintain or recover physical fitness.

Since starting distance running, I have jogged in 26 states of the U.S., and have run races in 14 states and in Ontario, Canada, England and Puerto Rico. In Kansas, I have raced in Hays, Hill City, Quinter, Ellis, Wakeeney, La Crosse, Collier, Hoxie, Gove, Oakley, Oberlin, Colby, Lawrence, Atwood, Scott Lake, McPherson and Topeka. By the end of the 20th century, many of the organized races in western Kansas had been dropped. They were continued in the larger cities, and Colby, Lawrence and Atwood are among those which have continued to have races in the new century.

My ribbons, medals and trophies came after age 74, and many of my medals are records in National Senior Olympics. Most of the runners in these races were 15 to 20 years younger than I, but I didn't usually finish last until about my middle 80s.

My most challenging event was a 10-mile run when I was 80. Even though I came in last, I set a national record for my age. My time was 1 hour, 44 minutes, 4.6

seconds. This was a national record for only a few weeks, but has remained a Kansas state record into the 21st century.

I look forward to the time when that record will be broken. But many of the 50 and 60-year-olds with whom I have raced, and who could beat that record when they are 80, have dropped out of racing by their seventies. Some day a runner with more diligent training than mine will break my record. I wonder if I will live to see that day, or will runners let me die with that record? Records are made to be broken.

I have to admit that a slowing does occur. Most of the races I entered were five miles or 10K (6.2 miles) In the numerous races I entered, I never came in last in my earlier years of racing. In my middle 80s, I began to slow down until I usually was last to finish. Diligent training ceased to improve my times. I then started entering two-mile runs or race walks. In my middle 90s I could walk three miles about as fast as I could run it. My workouts turned into mostly walking. My running changed to less than a lap around the track. I got no sympathy when I complained about my slowness, because most people thought I should be happy in being able to run at all. I talked to a Florida man who has run several marathons. He said his slowing down started in his 70s.

A couple months before I qualified as a centenarian, my wife Vernice and I entered a 1.24 mile race walk in Colby, Kansas. I started out good, but when I slowed my pace, Vernice passed me even though she questioned whether or not she should do that to me. As she looked back to see if she should wait for me, I waved her on and she beat me. (She lacks 12 years of being my age.) I was going as fast as I wanted to go. I take consolation because I can beat her out of bed in the morning and sometimes get breakfast! I'm glad she could beat me, because it helps me with my humility.

People are astonished to see a centenarian walking,

not driving, several blocks to the post office and office. A friend told me that when his father reached 90, he thought he was old, and started acting like it, and soon died. "Use it or lose it" is a slogan that has a lot of truth to it.

Running and other exercise programs, along with good lifestyle practices, should extend one's health and life span. Genes, according to some recent opinions, have only 30 percent of the influence on life span. The other 70 percent comes from lifestyle factors mostly under our control. My object has been to live a lifestyle that would permit me to be useful into old age, not necessarily to extend my life.

What was the effect on my fellow racers? What did it do for the racers much younger than I who finished behind me? I hope it didn't discourage them. Some, I know, were challenged to train to beat me, and some did, in later races. Some might have been encouraged by seeing that age is not the reason for people to lose the ability to run or participate in other strenuous exercise.

Chapter 7

WINNING GOLD

MY NATIONAL AND international competition started when I was 88, and shifting from distance running to shorter distances and race walking.

Before one race, we met a man who was coaching race walkers each week in Albuquerque. He gave me pointers on race walking which followed some peculiar rules that were enforced by disqualifying walkers. One of the rules was that the leg must be straight when directly under the body. The rule has since been changed to requiring a straight leg on the impact of the heel.

Another requirement was that the toe should be up 30 to 45 degrees on impact. I was somewhat perturbed that I had been walking for 90 years and wasn't doing it right. I tried to conform to the race rules and wasn't disqualified (DQD). My time was 12:49.49 in the 1600 meter race walk, which was good for a gold medal, with no competition in my age group. In my regular walking practices I don't follow race walk standards completely.

In the 1993 Senior Olympics at Baton Rouge, Louisiana, I had a competitor, Red Hall, from Oklahoma, in the 100 meter dash. I started the race slowly to avoid the possibility of pulling a ham string, but won the race at 24:06.

When I decided to compete in National Senior Olympics, my convictions regarding not running on Sunday caused me some inconvenience. They required athletes to qualify in a state Senior Olympics, and my chosen events were often scheduled on Sunday in Kansas. Therefore, I went to Tulsa, Oklahoma, for qualifying, since their events ended on Saturday. But the next year, they changed to Sunday, so then we went to Pierre, South Dakota, to qualify. Theirs ended with a banquet Saturday noon. There has been no stir about my refusal to run on Sunday, and I have not made a big deal about it. I regret that the athletic world is taking over the Sabbath, which was given to us for other purposes (rest and worship).

I decided to enter World Athletics Championship competition, which required no qualifying events. So I went to Buffalo, New York, in 1995, to the games in Gateshead, England, in 1999, and to Puerto Rico in 2003.

When I planned to go to the World Veterans Championships in England, I expected to have more competition in the "above 95" group, because the Europeans take more interest in track and field events than people in this country. Only one man competed with me, and that was in only the 5K (3.1 miles) race walk. His name is Julius Z. Spielberg, from Michigan. My race age was 96, and my opponent's 95. I had no competition in the 200 meter dash, discus or javelin.

At warm-up time I noticed a man on the track with a 95 on his identification tag. I asked him if he was Julius, and he said "yes." In our conversation I told him my goal in the 5K race walk was to make it in under 50 minutes. His goal was under 60 minutes. Mr. Spielberg had earlier in the year won a gold medal in the 5K race walk in the National Senior Olympics in Orlando, Florida. He introduced me to his three sons and some grandchildren. All my support group except my wife, Vernice, had departed for home.

We were the only walkers that were above 80 in age. As I was about to finish the race, I noticed that I would have to slow down or pass my opponent while he had a lap to go. I hated to lap him, because he had so many of his family to observe it. It is not customary to slow down for that purpose, so I lapped him. I learned that the correct pronunciation of lap in England is "lop." So I "lopped" my friend. My time was 57:06.80, and his was 1:02:25.70.

The other exciting event for me was the 200 meter dash. I was placed with the younger runners. One of them fell out of the race at about halfway. I was met at the end of the race by a lady who gave me a kiss on both cheeks! Vernice, my wife, came down out of the bleachers to get into the act. Then the lady, Kelly Ferrin, asked me a lot of questions, while reporters listened. She had written a book about old people — some were still in their 70s. She sent me some pictures and I bought her book, entitled *What's Age Got To Do With It?* Her home is in Carlsbad, California, and she was in England to take pictures.

I lost interest in the javelin because it didn't fly very far for me. The discus did better, making a world record, and they both got me gold medals, making a total of four.

Gold medals are hard to win unless you outlive your competitors. The medals were few, compared to the 6,000 athletes who hoped to take one home. Gold medals are also dangerous to wear around the neck. I found this out after a race at Syracuse, New York, when a woman grabbed me and hugged me while I was wearing a medal!

I celebrated my 100th year in July 2003, with a trip to the World Athletics Championships in Carolina, Puerto Rico. There were no other men over 95 in my events. My oldest competitor was eight years younger than I. It is easy to earn gold medals when one has no competition in one's age group!

In summarizing the winnings, the August issue of *National Masters News* stated, " 'Last but not least' is an understatement for Waldo McBurney of USA, who ran a World Record 100, put the shot three feet better than the previous record, and topped it all off with a U.S. record in the 5000 M race walk."

The shot put record was a big surprise to me. I didn't whirl around like the trained shot men do. The man conducting the event showed me a better form than I was using. I wondered if coaching was permitted in such an occasion. I was in an age class all my own, as all the other competitors were in a younger age group.

After one of my tries, I fell down as I turned to leave the ring, and skinned my nose. My humiliation was increased because my fall was caught on video by John Forman, my stepson. After three puts, I took no more because I didn't think I could do any better. And I didn't want to run the chance of humiliating myself again. The distances I made were far short of the 21 feet 4 inches that I made at a similar event 10 years earlier in Buffalo, New York. I was disappointed by my poor performance. I recovered when I read in the August issue of *National Masters News* that I had bettered the previous record by three feet. My record was 13.5 feet, or 4.12 meters.

The 5000 meter (3.1 mile) race walk was a slow event. In my heat were three men in the 85 to 89 age group. The oldest was 12 years younger than I, so I lagged several laps behind them. One of the officials told me to walk close to the left side of the lane, near the curb. I suppose that was so the faster walkers could pass me more easily. A sports medicine doctor walked with me the last few laps. He told me to walk in the middle of the lane. He probably noticed that I didn't walk a straight line, and thought I might hit the curb and fall or that I might be wobbling because I was weakening. I walked the last laps faster than the first ones. I wasn't aware of this, and wouldn't have believed it without my lap records. My doctor friend told me I gave him a good workout. My time was a slow 104.15.74, which was good for a U.S. record.

The younger runners in the 100-meter dash left me, with my 100-year-old body, far behind. Yet I heard my name, "Waldo!" chanted in the stands. My time was 38.02 and good for a world record. At the end of the race, people were waiting for my autograph. Others wanted the experience of shaking hands with a 100-year-old, and some just offered congratulations. Even a kiss on both cheeks was an occasional event. Some received satisfaction in merely touching a gold medal. It seems odd that the slowest performer of the approximately 4,000 athletes in competition in this world-wide contest should receive such a reception. It is, of course, in recognition that not many 100-year-olds are caught up in such odd behavior!

My wife, Vernice, age 88, entered the 100 meter dash. A 93-year-old woman, Igirias Rosario, from Mexico, was threatening to pass her. Vernice decided she shouldn't let an older runner beat her, so she picked up her pace. In doing so, she beat my time by two seconds, and she won a bronze medal. If we had been in the same heat, I would have tried to beat her.

The Puerto Rico medals are in three colors and the most beautiful we have ever seen. Medals are sought by over 4,000 great athletes who go home without one. World records were made in 27 events — 14 by women and 13 by men. Two of those were mine. I'm sure that hundreds worked harder than I did, and failed to get a gold medal.

We appreciated the courtesies of the Puerto Rican officials and people. It was a pleasure to be with them.

The old soddy — women wore bonnets in those days.

Editor is in picture, but was not born until a few weeks after the move. White object in Mother's hands is bust of Abraham Lincoln which rested on the roll-top desk.

Harvesting wheat with header and header barge — before days of combine — 1914 or 1915.

Harvest crew, 1914 or 1915. Wendell McBurney, second from right, died December 25, 1915. Others in photo: Lloyd McElroy, Melville or George Robb, Bert McElroy, Charles Graham and others not identified.

Both are Waldo, taken three minutes apart during the 75th anniversary of Beloit, Kansas, in the '30s.

Wagons Ho, outfit owned by Frank and Ruth Heffner. Ride across God's country on the trail the pioneers traveled across Kansas under threat of Indians.

Left: Checking winter feeding.

Nailing on entrance reducers to keep out the winter cold.

Curious great-grandchildren.

Grandpa Waldo giving bee les-
son to step-grandson Timothy
Forman.

Timothy is getting married in
early June 2004.

Left: Drying
painted hives.

Quick winter
inspection.

44

Big crop of honey on a high rainfall year. A couple of colonies made over 300 pounds of honey.

Lunch break at Sheridan Lake near bee yards.
Photo by Risto I. Routti from Finland.

45

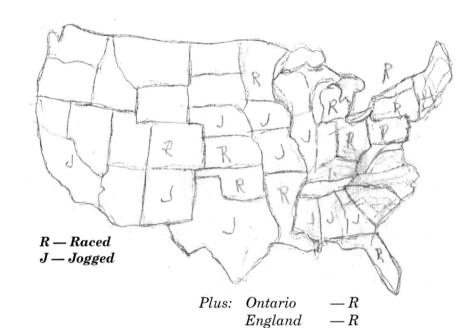

R — Raced
J — Jogged

Plus: Ontario — R
England — R
Puerto Rico — R

A race finish — in my 90s.

*Gold Medal salute —
Buffalo, New York,
1997.*

*Long jump,
age 90 —
Senior Olympics,
Baton Rouge,
Louisiana.
Distance: 7'4.5".*

*On TV.
Rocking chair
purchased after
tornado in 1880s.
Blanchard, Iowa,
maternal grand-
parents (Joseph
Huston).*

Great-grandchildren can't miss races.

Cobra Rock at Castle Rock south of Quinter, Kansas. It collapsed for the new century. Now just a heap of rock.

Waldo with Scott Huffman, world-wide pole vault performer. Quinter's world class athletes, 1996.

Dust storm in Quinter, KS 5/29/04; submitted by Tom Brockelman; taken by his daughter-in-law, Kim Brockelman.

48

What brought this on? *Questions after 200-meter dash in England, 1999.*

Folly of prophecy: Waldo didn't die in the 1900s.

Waldo and Vernice's celebration of 40th anniversary and Waldo's 100th birthday, July 2002.

Right: Waldo and Vernice McBurney's 40th anniversary.

100th birthday cake.

Photo by Gene and Ruth Spear.

50

Tom Forman, stepson, and Vernice and Waldo McBurney at races in Puerto Rico, July 2003.

A gold medal and a kiss, Puerto Rico, 2003.

Celebrating three gold medals at age 100, Puerto Rico.

Waldo and Vernice with Puerto Gold Medals.

In center background, note trophy for oldest participant in Kansas Senior Olympics.

Above: Waldo, Vernice and stepson, John Forman, in rain forest in Puerto Rico in 2003 while at the racing events. Hike more challenging than three-mile race walk.

Right: Shearing an upright red cedar at 100 years of age. Soon cut down — too tall for an old man's care. One of the neighbors drove around the block to see if the old man had fallen yet.

USA TODAY

Life

SECTION D

Monday, February 23, 2004

WALDO McBURNEY, 101;
by Chris Landsberger for USA TODAY.

Life at 101

An active lifestyle is key. More tips on long living.

The secrets to longevity

Genes may play a part, but so does lifestyle

By Kathleen Fackelmann
USA TODAY

Waldo McBurney ran the 100-meter dash at the World Masters Athletics Championships in Puerto Rico in July. He came in last.

Of course, at his age McBurney was lucky to compete at all. He was 100 at the time.

McBurney, now 101, thinks he's too slow to run in the next World Masters race. But who knows? McBurney never let his age stop him.

"I took up distance running when I was 65," he says.

McBurney is part of a study trying to unravel the secrets of extreme old age. Findings from the New England Centenarian Study in Boston suggest that longevity does run in families — the sibling of a centenarian is four times more likely to live past 90 than the general population.

But good genes are just part of the story.

Research from this study and others suggests that lifestyle plays a huge role in keeping the body and mind in top shape well into the eighth and ninth decade of life, says Thomas Perls, an aging expert at Boston University School of Medicine and study director.

Many of the centenarians in the study blew the top off the common assumption that old age must be filled with pain and disability.

"I started to slow down in my late 80s," McBurney says. Slowing down for him still includes a daily mile-long walk to his office in Quinter, Kan., where he runs a business that produces about 7,000 pounds of honey each year. He drives a car, works in his garden, and he's still tending about 100 colonies of bees.

Perls found that many of the superagers in his study had lived well past 90 without the disabling symptoms of heart disease, diabetes or even Alzheimer's. Of course, researchers can offer no guarantee that people who make lifestyle changes will live to age 100. But this study's findings suggest that most people can live well past 65.

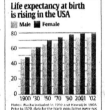

Life expectancy at birth is rising in the USA

■ Male ■ Female

Notes: Alaska included in 1959 and Hawaii in 1960. Prior to 1970, data for the black population were not available. 2002 data preliminary.
Source: National Vital Statistics Reports, Centers for Disease Control and Prevention

By Marcy E. Mullins, USA TODAY

Trophy life: McBurney has won numerous awards for track and shot put. He took up distance running when he was 65.

53

Chapter 8

WARNING SIGNAL

SINCE BOTH MY father and mother died of strokes, I thought strokes would be my old age problem. My father lived a slowed-down life for 30 years after his first strokes. My mother lived to the age of 83, and died after her second stroke.

At age 94, one night I had a pain in my left shoulder, so I got up and read until daylight. Then I went outside to scoop a 10-inch snow off the sidewalk. I came into the house sweating, and told my wife, Vernice, that I didn't have an appetite for eating breakfast. Soon, pain developed in my upper chest. Vernice suggested that I go to the doctor. "I'm ready now," I said. She gave me an aspirin, the third one I had taken in my life, and the first one without doctor's orders.

Vernice hurried to scoop the snow off the car and driveway, came back in the house and slipped on the kitchen floor with icy boots. It injured her shoulder, which later led to surgery and many months of therapy and pain., but that's another story.

She drove me to the hospital. The administrator, Paul Davis, was scooping snow off the entrance steps. I asked him where to go with a shoulder and chest pain. A nurse nearby said, "I'll show you," and led me to the waiting room. In a few minutes she led me to another room, where four or five nurses soon had me "wired up." By that time my doctor, Dan Lichty, appeared and after a little checking said, "We have a heart attack on hand."

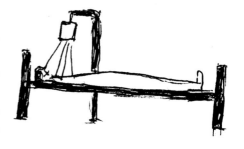

They wheeled me to a room near the nurses' station, and gave me a little stronger treatment than is usually given to old people, explaining that they thought I was in such good physical shape that I could handle it. I was in the hospital seven days. While there, I had pseudo-arthritic gout, which showed up with pain and swelling in the right knee and big toe.

A few weeks after release, I vomited blood, fainted, and went back to the hospital for five pints of blood and a nine-day stay at the hospital. Apparently the bleeding was caused by the medications which I had been taking to prevent blood clots and to relieve the gout.

The staff gave me excellent care in the hospital. They were courteous and caring. I commend everything but the food, which was not the kind that helped keep me out of the hospital for cardiac trouble for 94 years. It was tasty, and it probably pleased the tastes of most patients. But it was not the low-cholesterol, high-fiber, low-fat diet which I had been trying to follow at home.

Friends in the community were shocked that I would have a heart attack. How could a model of good health have such trouble? But, of course, runners are not invincible. Why me, when I expected that a stroke would be my warning signal? When I looked over my exercise record, it showed that in the last six months before my heart attack I had slacked off on my walking and running. I had harvested and processed 13,000 pounds of honey, which is strenuous exercise, during the previous summer and fall. I also walked about a mile a day, going to and from the office and post office, when I didn't need the pick-up truck for hauling things. This exercise was only one-quarter mile at a time, which is good but does not qualify for good aerobic exercise. About 30 minutes at one time is better. I concluded that I should be more diligent with my exercise program.

My cholesterol has never been very high, but the ratio of good cholesterol to bad cholesterol is not what it should be for safety from a heart attack and stroke. For several months before the heart attack I had been taking antioxidant pills containing vitamins C, E, beta carotene and selenium, and many other vitamins and minerals. Recent research indicates that homocysteine should be studied in relation to heart attacks. Having read reports of this research, I have responded by taking vitamin and mineral supplements containing vitamin B6, folic acid, and vitamin B12, which reportedly lower homocysteine in most cases.

I have heard much of scooping snow causing heart attacks. My doctor says my heart attack was at 3 a.m, when I had the shoulder pain, and not at 7 a.m. when I was scooping snow. That tells me that my trouble came at the time when my pulse was weakest and slowest, and not from vigorous exercise.

In explaining why the pain showed up in the back of my shoulder first, Dr. Lichty told me that the heart sends a pain message to the brain, but the heart does not record the pain in the heart. Therefore the message returns to other parts of the body. My first self-diagnosis of the shoulder pain was a pinched nerve. When the chest pain came, I immediately became suspicious of heart trouble. Stroke clinics are common in our community. Why not have heart clinics to explain how pains in shoulder, back or arms should be considered suspect?

The outcome of the heart attack, according to my doctor, was that no permanent damage was done. He relied mostly on me to bring about recovery of strength by my own therapy. That means that I have to be more faithful in my exercise program, taking multi-vitamin and mineral pills and, of course, a diet low in fat and high in fruits, vegetables, whole grain cereals and beans. I took the heart attack as a warning that I should be more diligent in observing a lifestyle that promotes my health. Prevention is my game.

Chapter 9

GROWING NUTRITION

WHEN A KID, I was called a gardener. Raising a garden has been a life-long hobby. Seeing things grow in straight, weedless rows is a joy. (That same tendency to good order does not transfer to my office desk or bedroom dresser, unfortunately!)

In recent years, we have had over 30 different fruits, vegetables and herbs growing in our garden and yard. Our favorite garden vegetables are tomatoes, green beans, carrots, cabbage, onions, cantaloupes, watermelons and peppers. Other crops on our list are okra, cucumbers, squash, spinach, garlic, parsley, potatoes, sweet potatoes, raspberries, peaches, apples, sweet corn, eggplant, and more. We often have seven different fruits and vegetables on the table at one meal. They come fresh out of the garden without shelf-life deterioration, or possible pesticide pollutants.

Our vegetables and fruits furnish vitamins, minerals and fiber that are good for health, including the eyes. Some could even function in ways similar to prescribed medicines. An example is garlic. One of its active ingredients is allicin, which is found in many drugs prescribed to lower cholesterol. Over two billion dollars' worth of these drugs were sold in 1993. *(Forbes Magazine,* 4-24-95.) Why don't doctors tell their patients that they can eat garlic (or other natural foods) instead of buying expensive medication to get the same active ingredients or benefits? There are many complex reasons, including FDA approval, liability concerns, dosages, lack of reliable nutrition education for doctors, and patients' expectations.

My son Kenneth took up gardening as a 4-H Club project when ten years old. We paid him half of the store price of the vegetables we ate. The records he kept were the basis of our payments. He became enthused with gardening and took over our family plot when he was in high school. Ken was chosen as the Kansas 4-H Club garden champion in 1948. When in college, he mailed home a garden plan for us to follow. He has continued gardening throughout his adult life.

Friends have insisted that the garden would not pay for the cost of irrigation water it requires. I answer, "Neither does golfing." Gardening takes the place of golf and other activities for me. It is better exercise than watching television after the evening meal!

Many times our garden furnished products not available at the store until recent years. The book, *Starving America,* showed my parents the importance of proper foods back in 1916. It was a plus for me, beginning with my youth in building a healthy body, and maintaining it in later years. I don't remember who I am quoting when I repeat, "You are what you eat."

In my early days of adulthood the extension horticultural specialist taught the value of home gardens. One statement made was that people without a garden do not eat enough fruits and vegetables for their health, even though they can afford to buy them.

My conclusion is that our gardens have not only paid well for the water, but have richly paid off in my health, and the health of my family.

Chapter 10

LOSING AND GAINING

"Even if I lose, I win." This is a statement of Dudley Rowe, age 82, of Washington, Iowa, made to one of his doctors as he was going into heart surgery. This statement came through his pastor, Rev. Douglas W Comin, and indicates that Mr. Rowe had the gift of faith which gave him comfort and confidence in this time of special stress and uncertainty of life. It reminds me of the scripture, Psalm 116:15, "Precious in the sight of the Lord is the death of His godly ones." Another comforting scripture is Psalm 23:4, "Even though I walk through the valley of the shadow of death, I fear no evil, for Thou art with me." Notice, it says *"through* the valley," not *into* the valley of death. It is comforting that, as Christians, we go through death into a life that is glorious beyond imagination.

An experience common to all people is death — of loved ones or friends, and finally, of oneself. Each person responds differently, but it is difficult in every case. In my lifetime, I have lost someone in almost every type of family relationship — parents, spouse, sister, brothers, daughter, grandchild and great-grandchild. Each loss has affected me differently. I often wondered how I would find comfort in the time of death. When a loved one dies, those who are left grieve the loss, but we know that the one who died has gained eternal joy and peace with the Lord.

My first experience with losing someone was when my older brother, Wendell, died at the age of 17, on December 25, 1915. The doctor listed the illness as bronchitis, but we called it pneumonia, because a nurse who helped care for him, Emma Robb (Mrs. G.M. Robb), thought it was pneumonia. He died without being seen by our doctor. In those days doctors made visits to homes, because there were no hospitals nearby.

This was a sad experience for me. I had tears for a year afterward whenever I would think about it. One of the letters we received quoted a scripture verse which I have never forgotten. Romans 8:28 reads, "All things work together for good to those who love God, who are called according to His purpose." Although it is often difficult to know the good that is to come, we trusted God to fulfill this promise. It was a great comfort to me.

The second death of a sibling in our family was my sister Beth (Mrs. Hugh Charles), at the age of 31, after just a few years of wedded life. Her disease was bacterial endocarditis. This was before sulfa and penicillin were recognized as antibiotics

At a family reunion in 1916, my father had a serious stroke. He lived 34 years after that. In his later years he became feeble, the farm in Quinter was sold, and my parents moved into a less demanding situation in Sterling.

Eventually, as he became more feeble, they moved into our home in Quinter, Kansas. Shortly afterward, he had another severe stroke which left him utterly helpless. He survived another year and a half, depending primarily on my mother for his complete care. For a period of time, my Aunt Jean McBurney, his sister, lived with us and helped. No rest home was available in our area in those days. He was as dependent on me as I had been on him in my infancy; yet in his weakness he still was to me an emblem of one who stood above me, remained my superior, and deserved my respect. He died in 1950 at the age of 88. I was at his bedside for his last breath.

My mother died several years later, at the age of 83. She had expressed the hope that she would not become an invalid and dependent on others, and that desire was fulfilled, as she died quickly and peacefully a few days after a stroke.

The recovery and the years after my father's second stroke impressed me with the value of nutrition. I thought it was all right to live to 88 like my father, but I wanted to live with health, strength and usefulness, and not slowed down like my father was.

One of my younger brothers, Paul, died of a heart attack at age 59. His wife, Caroline, had died earlier, soon after the birth of their only child, Beth. Also, Beth had died as a teenager in a fall off a cliff. Another older brother, Edwin, died at age 79, of strokes. Now, in 2004, from a family of six children, only two of us are still living — my younger brother Elmer, born in 1909, and I.

The next trial with death was the loss of Irene, my wife of 30 years. Our two older children, Kenneth and Ruth, were married, and the youngest, Mary Jane, was in college. The cause of her death was leukemia, for which no cure was known in 1960. Her passing was two months after diagnosis.

The husband and wife relationship is the closest relationship in human life. Therefore it is very stressful at separation time. Reading a book, *The Sovereignty of God,* by A.W. Pink, was a great help in preparing the two of us for the event of death. The book was a gift to us by A.D. Robb, a distant cousin and friend. We were reading the book separately before the diagnosis. After Irene became ill, I read it to her.

How could this book be of help to both of us at this time? A recent sermon by our minister, Rev. Steven Work, opened with these words, "The most hated and most comforting doctrine of the Bible is the sovereignty of God."

This doctrine is taught throughout the Bible, yet at this stage of world history many Christians reject it. In so doing, they miss the comfort it brings in crisis times of life, and in other less stressful times.

Some of the common emotional feelings at the time of death are shock, denial, anger, depression and guilt. By my recognition of God's sovereignty, I escaped these, for the most part. The most likely exception was slight depression. When I felt an inclination toward depression by feeling sorry for myself, how lonesome I was, etc., I would think of a Bible command, "In everything give thanks" (I Thessalonians 5:18). How can a person face death with thanksgiving? Some would insist that it is impossible. But I would turn my mind to the 30 wonderful years we had together, and the children God had given us. Simple obedience in being thankful headed off the tendency toward depression. I could say with Job, "The Lord gave and the Lord has taken away. Blessed be the name of the Lord" (Job 1:21). I trust God to do all things well, even if I can't understand how He will do it.

At the age of 34, my daughter Mary Jane (Mrs. Scott Boyle) and her baby daughter Tammy were killed in a tragic accident. About the same time, several in another family were also killed in an accident. The minister at the one funeral stated that it was not God's will that these people were killed. At the funeral of my daughter and granddaughter, the minister, Rev. Robert McFarland, taught that the deaths were in God's sovereign control and were for His glory.

At the memorial in Texas for his wife and daughter, Scott Boyle, her husband, met people at the door to cheer them. He trusted God's sovereignty and love. This Biblical teaching was a great comfort to him and he wished to pass it on to others.

My great-grandson, Michael Linders, was handicapped by leukemia from the age of two and a half until he died at age eight and a half, with some periods of remission. His second relapse meant it was a terminal case. He was deprived of many boyhood activities as the disease progressed. His Christian faith gave him assurance that his approaching next stage of life would be a glorious one. He influenced adults and youth to remember their Creator. His influence for good in his short life may have been greater than mine in 100 years of life.

God's sovereignty is truly a very comforting doctrine that has relieved me of a lot of stress. It is beyond my capacity to understand, but the Bible teaches it. I think I understand why it is the most hated doctrine of the Bible. "We the people" like to be in charge of everything. We don't like to surrender any power to any others. We don't like to accept anything we can't understand. I find God's sovereignty taught in the Bible from beginning to end. I can't understand it; neither can I understand why I keep breathing and wake up in the morning still alive! As I go to bed tonight, I trust that I will awaken in the morning if it is God's will and for His glory. Whatever is for His glory has to be acceptable to me.

How will I face my own death when that time comes, or prepare myself and my family?

Chapter 11

TRUSTING THE TRUSTWORTHY

WHEN I WAS a youngster, like all kids I put a lot of trust in my parents. They were the ones who could put things back together. I could lean on them for all solutions and childhood needs. My dad was a person above me whom I could respect and look up to. He had directed my life for good, and was my teacher, encourager, example and spiritual mentor. He and my mother taught us to put our full trust in the one true God, not just in them.

It is natural for human beings to look to some higher power. For Buddhists, it is an idol. For Indians, it might be the "great spirit." For some, it is money, health, power, a sport, or any number of things we wish to put first. For many, no time or place is given for anything outside of self. This, too, becomes a religion. Let's call it humanism. Everything is centered on self; anything goes as long as it pleases me. So we all encounter life with some kind of a god. They can't all be true gods. If it is from our own choosing, it is suspect, or just false.

Why should I be like the rooster who thinks he brings the sun up each morning by his crowing? All I would have to do to be like him would be to think of myself as all-sufficient in myself, with no need for any higher Power or greater knowledge than I possess. I have what I call my "11th Commandment," which is, "Don't take yourself too seriously." If I take myself too seriously, I am making myself my god, thus breaking the first commandment — "You shall not have any other gods before Me."

I chose the God who made me out of the soil. First, his plants grew to support animals, and my body was made of foods from both animals and plants. My God gave me eyes to see; I do not understand how. He gave me ears to hear, also senses of smell and taste. I have teeth to grind my food. Truly my body is "fearfully and wonderfully made." It is beyond my understanding. My conclusion is that I was created by a Being with great power and wisdom.

Some would have me believe that I was created by chance through a gradual process. I cannot accept that theory. That belief would give me no purpose in life, nor any responsibility in life except self. If my life just happened, I would be independent, not accountable to any creator for my acts, and life in general.

The God that I accept is One who created all things by His power and wisdom. A God who can create all things is one who can leave to man an instruction book which reveals Himself to man and what He requires of man. This I believe is revealed to us in the Holy Bible, containing the Old and New Testaments. This book has been preserved for us down through the centuries.

Why are we here? What is our purpose in life? Many years ago, a survey was made of soldiers to find their answers to these questions. Catholics and Jews seemed to be better prepared to answer, presumably because they had received more education in their creeds. The answer to those questions is given in the Westminster Shorter Catechism — " Man's chief end is to glorify God and to enjoy Him forever" (answer to question #1). Other catechisms give similar answers.

The God of the Bible reveals Himself as a God of three persons — God the Father, God the Son, and God the Holy Spirit. I cannot understand all the teachings of the

Bible, but I accept them in faith. I would feel guilty if I failed to study the message which God has prepared for me in His instruction book

If I had chosen a god of my own liking, with the attributes I liked, it would be a false god. The first commandment given in the Bible tells us Whom to worship, and the second tells us how to worship Him. The true God seeks and loves true worshippers. I try to fulfill these principles, though imperfectly.

My parents held family worship morning and evening, consisting of singing of Psalms, Bible reading and prayer. This practice I have carried on most of my life, except that we do it only in the morning. My understanding of the Bible and how I should obey its teaching have been helped by family worship, church worship, Bible class, personal study and conferences. My knowledge of the Bible is still incomplete, and it is worthy of a lifetime of study.

My church, the Reformed Presbyterian Church of North America, practices singing Psalms exclusively and without instruments. Most Christian churches reject these standards. They are not popular. Are they right according to the Bible? I think so. God has given us the book of Psalms in the Bible to help us in His worship and praise. The worship in my church is far from perfect, but we try. We are not a museum of saints, but a church of repentant, converted sinners. God seeks worshippers to worship in spirit and in truth. He is very particular about His worship

What if I had never read the Bible or studied it? It has been preserved for me down through the ages to introduce me to my Creator. We thank our friends for favors and gifts. What if I gave no thanks or praise to my Creator Who gave me His Word? To Him I owe thanksgiving, praise, honor, loyalty, faith and obedience. To neglect Him in this is rebellion and sin, which makes me deserving of His righteous punishment.

Since we all have sinned in many ways, God has graciously provided for us to be forgiven. This is through His Son, Jesus Christ, Who took the punishment we deserve, by dying on the cross and rising again.

Chapter 12

HONORING OTHERS

WHAT DOES HONOR have to do with length of life?

I was a feisty little rebel as a kid. My older brothers didn't always treat me in the right and honorable brotherly way. At least, sometimes I didn't think so. When I thought that my older brother Edwin was unfair with me, I had a quick way of setting him straight — that was by sinking my teeth into his shoulder! That controlled him, but my mother interfered. She gave me a knife and sent me out to the peach trees to get a switch to use on me. I felt punished all the way out and all the way back, and especially when I got back! My mother's method of punishment must have worked. I haven't bitten anyone in over 90 years! Parents in those days didn't know about "spankless" punishments, nor had they heard much about child abuse.

I am thankful for parents who taught me right and wrong with the switch when that was deemed appropriate. Parents now are taught other methods of discipline such as time-outs and sitting in the corner. Those are good as long as they work, but it seems to me that on some occasions more drastic methods are appropriate and necessary. Has this "spankless" system brought less violence to our present society? Some now claim that a spanking (even if well-deserved) is violence and would therefore make the child violent. But when I check today's violence compared to the era of spankings, I have some doubts.

I was told a story that sounded true. A week of school had passed and one boy continued unacceptable behavior. The teacher decided "time is up" and he used a switch. The next morning the dad came to school and asked the teacher why he had whipped his son. The teacher replied, "I whipped him because you don't whip him at home, and if you don't whip him at home, I'm going to whip him at school." The dad returned home.

The fifth commandment in the Bible is "Honor your father and mother" — but that isn't all of it — "so that you may live long in the land the Lord your God is giving you." This is the only promise of long life in the ten commandments. God knew that a person who did not honor his parents would live in conflict, rebellion and stress.

The fifth commandment requires us to have proper relationships with our superiors, our equals and our inferiors, according to the interpretation of Scripture as summarized in one widely known book of biblical instruction, the Westminster Shorter Catechism. So the commandment means that we should honor not only our parents, but people in all other relationships. If I had been rebellious toward my parents and hadn't learned to honor them, I would likely have had the same bad relationships with other people. I would have rebelled against my brothers, sister, teachers, fellow students, co-workers, employers, superiors, and those under my supervision. My life would have been in conflict if I hadn't learned honor at home. My conflict would have brought stress, and stress is not healthy and tends to shorten one's life.

My father always insisted on our treating our mother and him with respect, honor and obedience. The idea of running away from home never entered my mind, and I think the same was true of all my brothers and sister.

The family was ordained by God. He made the husband the head of the home and holds him responsible for it. He instructs wives to be subject to their husbands, and husbands to love their wives (Ephesians 5:22-28). This made it very necessary that I choose a wife that I can love and honor, and that I should be a husband worthy of her submission. I have not been a perfect husband or father, but it has been a challenge to strive for that goal. This instruction in Ephesians doesn't mean that the husband is to lord it over his wife, and if he loves her he will not do so. Unworthy husbands and unworthy wives have broken up many homes and brought much sadness to them.

I have concluded that there is no such thing as two perfectly compatible people. For two people to get along together there must be give and take. My policy is that in the kitchen, my part is mostly in an "advisory" capacity; in bee management, I cast the majority vote!

My long life does not prove that I have kept this commandment perfectly, but I have tried.

Chapter 13

LEARNING FROM CREATURES

OATS AND BARLEY have gained respect as human food, especially oat bran. I am reminded of the story of early dictionaries. The English dictionary defined oats as food for horses in England, and food for people in Scotland. The Scottish dictionary answered by defining oats as food for horses in England, and for people in Scotland, and added that England produced horses and Scotland produced men!

In the 1940s, my family was in the business of turkey production, as a sideline. It was year-round, including the laying flock and incubation. It was our goal to have turkeys past the pin-feather stage in time for the Thanksgiving market. To do this, we were advised to feed them oats. In case oats was not available, we could get the same results with barley.

In order to have hatchability in turkey eggs, the laying turkeys must have animal protein supplement. Our feed-mixer included fish meal in laying feed to furnish this nutrient. We hatched eggs for another turkey grower who didn't feed fish meal. The eggs hatched well because their turkeys followed cattle. Cattle make their own vitamin B-12, which is the vitamin contained in animal protein. It is excreted in the manure, which was then available to the turkeys. Instead of using the term "animal protein supplement," we now call it Vitamin B-12.

When I was working as the county extension agent, a call from a feed dealer asked me to see what was wrong with his baby chicks. They could hardly stand up and walk. I diagnosed the problem as lack of vitamin D. I told him that the feed producer had evidently missed getting the vitamin and mineral supplement in his batch of feed. He took his feed to a local elevator, where a double amount of supplement was added. Others around the elevator got to calling the manager "Doc" for thinking he could cure sick chickens! In answer to this teasing, the manager made a telephone call to see how the chicks were doing. The answer was that they had fully recovered and were doing fine. The feed company made adjustments for their error.

Sheep growers in 1950 had been informed that vitamin E had increased the conception of ewes by 14 percent. Some sheep men like to produce lambs ready for the Easter market because it is usually the high price time of year. I fed ewes wheat in order to give them the vitamin E in the germ. The ewes lambed in the fall instead of in the spring, which is normal for sheep.

Experiences with livestock and poultry have helped me to realize the importance of food for my health. Farmers and stockmen are aware of the importance of vitamins, minerals and proteins in feeds. It has long seemed to me that information on livestock feeding was more reliable and better accepted than material published on human nutrition. Commercial prejudices often warp sound information. It has been one of my great problems in human nutrition to sort out truth from error.

We know a lot of facts that are not proved by research beyond the probable error. We can be over-skeptical in accepting ideas published on nutrition. Doctors must be cautious, and in so doing they avoid a lot of heresies, but at the same time they miss a lot of truths.

We accept the fact that water expands when it freezes, while most things expand as they warm up. We believe these facts without citing a research project that proves them.

Many people claim good results from bee venom therapy for multiple sclerosis and some kinds of arthritis. The medical profession can't recommend them because acceptable research has not been done. The research hasn't been done because nobody is going to spend a million dollars on bee venom therapy, because bee stings can't be patented, and you can't make money on drugs without a patent.

Turkeys balance their food perfectly. That is, if they are fed grains and protein-rich feed separately, they will eat the proper proportions. Lightweight breeds of chickens have this ability better than the heavy breeds. People aren't like turkeys. We tend to eat foods that taste good. So we eat too much fat, too much protein, too much sugar and too much salt. We tend to eat too little fruit, vegetables, whole grain cereals and legumes. Then we don't exercise enough. All sorts of ailments come to us as a result of these habits. A high percent of our physical ailments may be caused by our food, and lack of exercise.

When questioned about why I eat a food that isn't so good, I answer, "because I like it!" We have to learn to like some foods that are good for us. I liked peas better after I learned that they are rich in vitamins and minerals. Some foods require more effort to learn to like them — such as parsnips and asparagus.

Some nutritionists say that fruits and vegetables contain all the salt we need and that we eat 10 times as much salt as we need. We have reduced the use of salt on our table. When working in the sun in 100-degree weather, I have had leg cramps at night. I didn't get relief from the common trace minerals, but taking some extra salt stopped the cramps. I have concluded that those who think vegetables and fruits contain all the salt we need must live in an air-conditioned house and drive an air-conditioned car to an air-conditioned workplace. Their recommendation didn't work for me when I worked in hot weather. Yet many people lower their blood pressure by reducing salt intake.

Chapter 14

BEES CAN READ

MAN CAN CLEARLY see that there is a creator. "There are no atheists in foxholes," is a statement we hear, especially in war times. This statement isn't altogether true.

Being a beekeeper, I can say that it would be very difficult for me to be an atheist. Bees are called creatures of instinct and have no reasoning power; yet they do so many amazing things. Bees are "chemists" that make the wax of highest melting point out of honey or sugar. They are "architects" that form this wax into hexagon-shaped cells that can store 20 times their weight in honey.

Bees are "heating engineers," that keep the brood temperature at 95 degrees F even when the temperature outside the hive is below zero, and even with an opening at both the top and bottom of the hive they live in. They cool the hive when it is hot by evaporating water and by fanning air through the hives with their wings.

Talk about flying by instrument — man has learned this in fairly recent history. Bees use similar activity in their existence. When a bee discovers a source of nectar, pollen or water, she reports it when she goes back to the hive. She performs a dance which tells other bees the direction and distance to its discovery. This direction is given according to the direction of the sun in the sky at the time. She gives directions inside the hive when she can't see the sun. She knows the direction of the sun even though she can't see it because she is sensitive to polarized light. (whatever that is.)

Bees give off odors (pheromones) that cause them to act in appropriate ways. One odor is the alarm odor which causes them to protect their hive (sting). Another leads them to assemble. The queen gives off an odor that affects the morale of the whole colony and puts them in a working mood.

Yes, and bees can read! The marks on the hives in this drawing are used by beekeepers to identify the hives when they are similar or close together. The bees find their home by these marks. I tell school kids that bees learn to read when they are only two weeks old and go outside of their home for the first time.

Bees don't cease to amaze me even though I have been a beekeeper for over 70 years. Bees have proved to me that they didn't just happen to come into being by some chance force. "For the invisible things of Him from the creation of the world are clearly seen, being understood by the things that are made, even His eternal power and Godhead; so they are without excuse" Romans 1:20.

I can't claim disbelief of anything I don't understand, or is not reasonable or hasn't been proven by approved research methods. If I had never managed bees, to observe them, I would still have my own body which is "fearfully and wonderfully made," as evidence of the Creator.

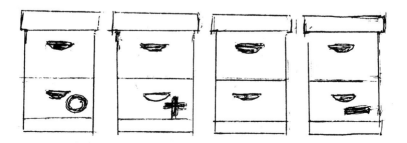

I can go to sleep even though I don't understand what makes that possible. I wake up in the morning still breathing and my heart is still beating. I don't know how these things continue, but I do know it is without my conscious effort.

I breathe air into my lungs, and oxygen goes through a membrane into my bloodstream, and then is distributed to all parts of the body, changed into carbon dioxide, returned to the heart in the blood, turned back into the lungs and exhaled. This process has taken place in my body all my life, and it is a marvelous process I can't understand.

This and dozens of other functions of my body are performed that are above my understanding. I came into existence through no effort or intention within me. If there were no other wonders in the world, my body would teach me that there is a great, wise and powerful creator God Who is responsible for the wonders I observe and work with daily.

Nearly every contraption we buy is accompanied by operating instructions. These we are supposed to study. I usually do it when all else fails. A God Who is powerful enough to create me and all else also has the power to give us an instruction book, teaching us what we are to believe concerning Him and what duty He requires of us. I accept the Holy Bible as this book of instruction. This book tells us what is good and what is bad. This book merits a life-long study. Great blessings are promised to those who obey the teachings of this book, and punishment to those who rebel against it.

The book teaches that God breathed into man a living soul that never dies. We are responsible for all of our actions and will meet our Creator at the end of this life, to face His righteous judgment, whether good or bad.

It was normal for me to come into this world as a selfish little rebel. The Good Book tells us how to overcome and have victory over this tendency. It is impossible for any person to live a perfect life. God the Father gave His Son, Jesus Christ, as a sacrifice to pay for the sins of those who trust in Him.

Chapter 15

WHO SAID IT FIRST?

"DID GOD SAY ...?" Yes, He did. He had much to say on many aspects of life. There are many biblical instructions that science has proved reliable. But *God said it first.*

For the first half of my life I don't remember any cautions from the media against eating animal fats. Now all the recommendations on food that I am acquainted with caution against eating too much fat. The heart and cancer authorities warn that too much fat, especially animal fats and hydrogenated fats, can be harmful in many ways. But I learned it first from the Bible. "You shall not eat any fat." Leviticus 3:17 was given to God's people several thousand years ago. Olive oil was a much-used oil in Bible times, and it is now recognized as a very beneficial oil. Present-day processing makes many vegetable oils harmful, like animal fats, because they are hydrogenated.

The Bible placed great importance on how we should think. We are told in Philippians 4:8, "Finally, brethren, whatever is true, whatever is honorable, whatever is right, whatever is pure, whatever is of good repute, if there is any excellence, and if anything worthy of praise, let your mind dwell on these things."

Again, we are told in I Thessalonians 5:18, "In everything give thanks." Impossible? After the death of my first wife, Irene, instead of feeling sorry for myself and brooding over my loss and loneliness, it was rewarding to think rather of those wonderful 30 years, and the children and other blessings the Lord had given us. "In everything give thanks" Impossible? Yet when following this command, even in my imperfect way, it brought me comfort in place of sorrow and depression. God has rewarded me for being obedient to this "impossible" instruction.

Anger, scientists say, produces an enzyme which raises blood pressure and makes us ready for "fight or flight." Continued anger is damaging to our bodies and may lead to heart problems or even death. "Do not let the sun go down on your anger," God told His people nearly two thousand years ago in Ephesians 4:6. *He said it first.*

Many doctors today say that a person with a poor prognosis, but a wholesome positive attitude, may be better off than a person in better physical condition but with a pessimistic attitude. A recent newspaper had an article entitled, "Research links pessimism to early-death risk." Laughter and humor have been recognized as being very beneficial to health. The Bible says, "A joyful heart is good medicine" (Proverbs 17:22). *God said it first.*

The media at the turn of the 21st century is reporting that churchgoers, and those who pray, have longer lives. God blesses and honors those who worship and glorify Him. Not all who go to church or pray are truly worshipping Him with their hearts and lives, however.

It has been said that the easiest way to shorten one's life is to do nothing. Another way that requires no physical effort is to worry. Worry is a killer. As hard as I try, I don't avoid all worry. The Bible says in Matthew. 6:25, "Do not be anxious for your life, as to what you shall eat, or what you shall drink, nor for your body, what you shall put on." This scripture says to take "no anxious thought," which means don't worry.

I have a mouse trap which lets its victims into a compartment which confines them. I have seldom taken a live mouse out of that trap, just dead ones that seem to soon worry or fret themselves to death.

Worriers have a lot of troubles in their lives, but most of them never happen! Worry shortens life and makes life miserable. It comes from lack of trust in God.

Chapter 16

SUMMING UP

How does a man over 100 continue beekeeping and winning gold medals in track and field events?

SOME POSSIBLE ANSWERS:
1. EXERCISE? Yes, of primary importance, and most easily neglected. My choice for many years has been running, but many other forms of exercise are beneficial.
2. NUTRITION? Yes — fruits, vegetables, whole grain cereals, beans, low-fat, low-salt, and low-sugar help control weight, and help prevent cancer, heart trouble, diabetes and many other diseases that shorten life. We tend to "dig our graves with our teeth."
3. WORK? Ten-hour days and six-day weeks were the standard in my early days. Heavy physical work was available. Today's boys have little chance for regular physical exertion, and some have their first taste of it in athletics. Hard work didn't hurt me — it helped.
4. REST? Neither body nor mind function properly without rest. "Six days you shall labor and do all your work, but the seventh day is a Sabbath of the Lord your God; in it you shall not do any work." — 4th commandment. I have tried to be faithful on the

Sabbath rest. In my lifetime I have spent 14 years of resting days.

5. GENES? Genes get blamed for a lot of ailments. Now we are told that only 30 percent of our health problems can be blamed on inheritance. Lifestyle is the more important factor. We don't get to choose our parents, but we can select our life-styles. Both of my parents died of strokes, so I have lived defensively against that trouble.

6. ANTIBIOTICS? My brother Wendell died of pneumonia, and my sister Beth died of bacterial endocarditis, before sulfa and penicillin came into use. Without these antibiotics I might have been dead long ago.

7. VITAMIN AND MINERAL SUPPLEMENTS? I was already old before I started taking supplements. As we get older, we eat less and do not utilize food as well as when younger. Eating good foods helped supply my needs. The processing of foods today removes many of the nutrients, so supplements are essential. Using antioxidants to control free radicals tends to reduce cancer and heart trouble.

8. WEALTH? Very handy! But it cannot produce good health. We lived many years on poverty-level income, but we ate as well or better than the wealthy, thanks to our home garden. When I came to retirement age, we had little more than a home and business. We trusted the Lord Who promised to supply all our needs. Some money we didn't earn was invested wisely, and it has grown until we can have anything we want. If I had been a worrier, I might have been dead before now.

9. STRESS MANAGEMENT? Stress not handled properly is a killer. I have tried to put my trust in the Lord.

10. POSITIVE ATTITUDE? If I think I can, I probably will.

11. PEACEFUL NATURE? Without peace we are under stress, which is a killer.
12. GOOD ETHICS? A liar isn't believed when he tells the truth. A thief can't sleep well day or night for fear of being caught. "A good name is to be more desired than great riches" (Proverbs 22:1).
13. FAITH? If my strength were in myself I would be a sure loser. My true strength is in the Lord Who made heaven and earth.
14. GIFT OF GOD? The Giver of all good and perfect gifts, the one in Whom we live and move and have our being.
15. MEDICAL DOCTORS? I would have been dead without the skill of medical doctors. My "game plan" is prevention and I have avoided doctors as much as possible, but when I needed them on several occasions, they saved my life.
16. CHIROPRACTORS? I might have been a cripple without them, and have found them to be knowledgeable on nutrition. Other "alternative" methods of treatment that I haven't used also have merit.
17. DENTISTS? Who can get along without them? My wisdom teeth were pulled in my 40s, for which I paid $3 each. I now have two root canals, and three or four fillings. I haven't been much of a consumer of candy, cookies, cake or pop. My teeth are worn short.
18. HONEY? The best sweetener contains nutrients, such as vitamins, minerals and enzymes, that are not found in other sweets. Honey is on the table every day in our home.
19. VINEGAR? Apple cider vinegar is reputed to have health benefits, especially for arthritis. It didn't add to my health, because I didn't use it constantly.
20. MOTIVATION? There is talk of the possibility of living to 120. I don't think I have motivation to do what would need to be done to reach that age. It takes strong incentives to eat the right foods, avoid the

junk foods, and exercise regularly. When I started entering races, it turned my fitness program into a sport, which provided the incentive I have needed as I have grown older.

21. MARRIAGE? Studies have concluded that married people live longer. I have lived 70 of my first 100 healthy years as a married man. God said, in Genesis 1:28, "It is not good for the man to be alone. I will make him a helper suitable for him."

Chapter 17

MY HALL OF FAME

IT HAS BEEN my privilege to come into contact with many world-famous people. These include master runners, but also some with great athletic achievements, and still others that meant much to me in many ways.

My parents, GEORGE ROBB McBURNEY and MARY BERTHA HUSTON McBURNEY, really earned first place in my Hall of Fame. Their good influence on me as a boy is beyond my ability to express. Their love for all their children made our home a place we always enjoyed. We were taught the ethics of the Bible and were encouraged to follow its teachings. Proper eating habits were taught.

IRENE McBURNEY, my college sweetheart, my wife and mother of our three children, holds a prominent place. She was a graduate in home economics from Kansas State College. She was well prepared to care for our family and lead in 4-H projects in food and clothing. She was an excellent mother, and trained our children with firmness, patience and love. She was an encouragement to me, and a most worthy helper in the 30 years that the Lord gave us together.

I can't leave out my wife, VERNICE McBURNEY, from my Hall of Fame list. Her encouragement, companionship and food preparation were factors in keeping me fit and healthy. My son, stepsons, daughter, grandchildren and at least one great-grandchild have jogged with me and given me great encouragement and satisfaction.

GLEN CUNNINGHAM is the first athlete on the list. He recovered from severe burns on his legs as a boy to become a world-famous runner and dominated the world in middle distance running for several years. His high school coach timed him on a sub-4-minute mile. They kept it a secret for many years for fear that no one would believe it. I saw him run the mile against a relay of four high school quarter-milers in Beloit, Kansas. He came out ahead of them. That was in the '30s. We had him in our home for a meal in the '50s, after we moved to Quinter.

JIM RYUN was the first high school boy to run a sub-4-minute mile, which in over 35 years has not been equaled. He won more high school, college, national and world records than any other runner in Kansas state history. I was in a three-mile race with him in Tampa, Florida. It was an out-and-back race. He was well on the way back long before I was "out." I had the privilege of meeting him in person in Colby, Kansas. At present, he is U.S. Representative for Kansas District 2.

ARNE RICHARDS, of Manhattan, Kansas, has to be in my Hall of Fame. He looked me up after a 10K race at Hays, and gave me words of encouragement. He influenced Bob Anderson to establish the Runners' World magazine. He died while on his run one morning.

JIM FIX was a runner whom I met when I was in a 10K race with him in Topeka, Kansas. His father died of a heart attack in his forties, and he also died at an early age (40s or 50s, I think.) He had the idea that all it took to postpone heart trouble was to run. It has taken a lot more than running to get me to age 94 for my first heart attack. If a fatal heart attack takes me, I would just as soon it would happen on a run or walk, as in a hospital.

BOB CREIGHTON, director of the Lake Atwood 10-

mile races for many years, made two statements that have impressed me enough that I can't forget him. As I was waiting for the Atwood 10-mile race to start, he told me that when I finished the race I would have a national record. I finished the race and had the record for a few weeks before it was broken. My record still stands as a Kansas record for age 80, at this writing.

He also told me that I had the potential of making world records. Frankly, I didn't believe him, but I didn't tell him so. After competing in National Senior Olympics in Syracuse, New York and Baton Rouge, Louisiana, I realized that he was right. I wrote a letter and told him so.

MARVIN STARK was a runner and race director for the Colby, Kansas, races. His good turn for me was making a class for 80-plus runners when other races had classes for 65-plus or 70 and over. He promised to go to 90-plus when the appropriate time would come, but he died before that time, and I became "just a walker" for most competitions. His daughter, Terri, ran with me on one of my last laps in the Atwood 10-mile after she had finished the race.

My encouragers at Hays, Kansas, races are numerous, but some I should mention are DR. PAUL WAGNER, CONNIE DREHER, MARILYN GINTHER and BOB MCANANY. They treated me like a real winner even though I finished with the bottom fourth of the runners.

There are many more runners and race officials that I should have in my Hall of Fame, since I have run in races in more than a dozen towns in Kansas. Since I can't cover them all, I hesitate to mention even a few. I have had words of encouragement from many race directors, participants and spectators.

MICHAEL AHEARN — "Mike," as everybody knew him — didn't win his fame in running, but he spent a lifetime at K-State U. as a coach and athletic director. As a football coach, he won two-thirds of his games. The

Ahearn Fieldhouse is named in his honor. He was also a teacher in the Horticulture Department in his early days. I had more contact with him than most students because I majored in horticulture.

Mike was known for his quick wit. When the apple-judging team took the train to a contest in Grand Rapids, Michigan, Mike happened to be on the same train. One of the team members said that the newspaper gave his home as "Layetta" instead of "Mayetta." Mike said, "They must have thought you were on the chicken judging team."

FOREST ("Phog") ALLEN, a long time coach at K.U., has to be in my Hall of Fame because he has been called the "father of basketball coaching." He was a great man even though he brought fame to K.U., the athletic arch-enemy of my school, K-State. I met him at an athletic banquet in my hometown of Quinter. He didn't hold it against me that I am a K-Stater.

JAMES NAISMITH invented basketball in 1892, at Springfield, Massachusetts. I had no direct contact with Naismith, but an indirect association — my landlady, Florence Kincaid, in Beloit, Kansas, when I first got out of college. Her husband died later and she moved to Lawrence where her son was going to school. She married Dr. Naismith. His hometown was Almonte, Ontario, Canada, and they were justly proud of him. Since my son Kenneth lived there for a number of years, I had the opportunity to get a ball point pen with his name on it. On the 100th anniversary of the invention of basketball, a dedication ceremony was held in Almonte for a plaque honoring Dr. Naismith. The Canadian Postal Service also participated with a commemorative stamp. Kenneth offered the prayer at the dedication ceremony. Two of my grandsons attended Naismith Elementary School, named in his honor.

LEE RAZAK was a blind runner who did his workouts in familiar territory without assistance. Marilyn

Ginther, and perhaps others, served as his guide in some races I observed in Collyer and Hays. I admired him because his handicap didn't keep him from healthful exercise.

HOMER COURTNEY, of Quinter, threw away his arthritis medications, which had caused him severe side effects, and started running. He finished a marathon in Herrington, Kansas, in his seventies.

Then there is DICK WILSON, who has numerous records to his credit. He made many records while living in Indianapolis and in his retirement years in Lawrence, Kansas. His wife was Joan Fink, a Quinter native. I once rode a bicycle as he ran on a five-mile workout at Quinter. I had to gain speed going downhill in order to beat him going up the hill. He is a super runner, and I have challenged him to break my 10-mile record when he reaches 80 years of age.

SCOTT HUFFMAN, as a world- famous pole vaulter whose home town is Quinter, should be near the top of my Hall of Fame list. His boyhood ambition was to break the pole vault record of his father, Galen Huffman, at McPherson College. Instead, he went to the University of Kansas, where he broke U.S. records. He is known in Europe for his unorthodox style known as the "Huffman roll." He holds the U.S. record at 19'7".

All-American football player VERYL SWITZER was a member of the Nicodemus 4-H Club under the leadership of Blanche White when I first knew him (when I was county agent in Hill City, Kansas). He was a leading player in the Bogue High School eight-man football team that was undefeated. Switzer was one of the three black athletes who broke open the opportunity for black athletes to participate in the Big Seven after entering Kansas State University, then KSAC. I remember him for his open-field running and as a safety that few ever passed by. He was the subject of abuse because of his race, which he endured without retaliation. That attitude gained him the respect of everyone. He played professional football and was a member of the KSU athletic department for many years.

ERIC LIDDELL, the "Flying Scot," has a place in this book because he and I have something in common (although I never had the privilege of meeting him). Eric said, "I'm not running on a Sunday," and I, too, have refrained from running on Sunday, the Lord's Day. Liddell, a Scotsman, became the top contender in the 1924 World Olympics in Paris, in the 100-meter dash. But it was scheduled to be held on Sunday, so he would not enter that race. That jarred his fans all over the United Kingdom. He was severely criticized and called a traitor to his country. On contest day, Liddell was preaching in Old Scots Kirk in Paris.

Liddell decided to run the 400-meter race, even though he had little time to train for this middle distance event. Near the end of the race he was two meters ahead of the nearest runner. He put on a kick and ended five meters ahead and won the Olympic title in a world record time of 47.6. Critics turned to praise the one whom they had scorned.

Soon after the Olympics, Liddell went to China as a missionary, and he died in a Japanese internment camp on February 21, 1945. His notoriety came at an early age. For more details, read *The Flying Scotsman,* by Sally Magnuson, or see the movie *Chariots of Fire.*

There are many who have influenced my life who are not included in this Hall of Fame. Why should I give preference to those who entered it through the athletic field? Many more could be recognized, such as fellow students, teachers, beekeepers, leaders in organizations I have labored in, 4-H club members and leaders, spiritual leaders and students I have taught, who had something to teach me. It is impossible to recognize all who have been an uplifting part of my life.

TRACK AND FIELD STATISTICS
R.Waldo McBurney
Box 277, Quinter, Kansas 67752
Phone: 785-754-3534

| Age 74 | 1977 | Ottawa, Ontario, Canada |
| Mile | 7:07 | Informal meet |

| Age 80 | 1983 | Atwood, Kansas |
| 10 mile | 104:04.6 | Kansas Record (U.S. record briefly) |

Age 88 1991   Syracuse, New York
Senior Olympics
    200 M .... :45.69
    800 M 4:46.30
    5000 M 43:59

Age 90 1993   Baton Rouge, Louisiana
Senior Olympics
    Long Jump .... 7'4.5"
    Shot Put .... 21'4"
    100 M .... :24
    200 M .... :47.54
    400 M 2:14.06
    1500 M Race Walk 12:49.49

Age 92 1995   World Masters, Buffalo, New York
    Triple Jump .... 4.04 M   Record
    Shot Put .... 6.70 M   Record
    High Jump .... .98 M   Record
    200 M 1:00.70
    800 M 5:50

Age 96 1999   World Masters, Gateshead, England
    Discus .... 13.56 M   World Record
    Javelin .... 9.52 M
    200 M .... 1:03.08   World Record
    5000 M Race Walk . 57:06.8   World Record

Age 100 2003   World Masters, Carolina, Puerto Rico
    Shot Put .... 4.12 M (13'5")   World Record
    100 M .... :38.02   World Record
    5000 M Race Walk 104:15.74   U.S. Record